Narrative Inquiry

POCKET GUIDES TO
SOCIAL WORK RESEARCH METHODS

Series Editor
Tony Tripodi, DSW
Professor Emeritus, Ohio State University

KATHLEEN WELLS

Narrative Inquiry

OXFORD
UNIVERSITY PRESS
2011

OXFORD
UNIVERSITY PRESS

Oxford University Press, Inc., publishes works that further
Oxford University's objective of excellence
in research, scholarship, and education.

Oxford   New York
Auckland   Cape Town   Dar es Salaam   Hong Kong   Karachi
Kuala Lumpur   Madrid   Melbourne   Mexico City   Nairobi
New Delhi   Shanghai   Taipei   Toronto

With offices in
Argentina   Austria   Brazil   Chile   Czech Republic   France   Greece
Guatemala   Hungary   Italy   Japan   Poland   Portugal   Singapore
South Korea   Switzerland   Thailand   Turkey   Ukraine   Vietnam

Published by Oxford University Press, Inc.
198 Madison Avenue, New York, New York 10016
www.oup.com

Wells, Kathleen.
Narrative inquiry / Kathleen Wells.
p. cm. — (Pocket guides to social work research methods)
Includes bibliographical references and index.
ISBN 978–0–19–538579–3 (pbk. : alk. paper)
1. Narrative inquiry (Research method) 2. Social service. I. Title.
H61.295.W44 2011   001.4'33—dc22

Printed in the United States of America
on acid-free paper

Acknowledgments

I thank the Mandel School of Applied Social Sciences at Case Western Reserve University for granting the sabbatical that launched my work on this volume; the University of Chicago School of Social Service Administration and Chapin Hall Center for Children and the University of Denver Graduate School of Social Work for the support those institutions provided during my sabbatical year; the Centre for Narrative Research at the University of East London for enabling my participation in the center's narrative research seminar; reviewers of the book proposal and a first draft of this manuscript, especially Ian Shaw, Corinne Squire, and an anonymous reviewer, each of whom read the first draft of the book in its entirety and whose evaluations were most helpful; and the many colleagues with whom I engaged in discussion of narrative inquiry writ large along the way.

This book is dedicated to the memory of my mother, Nell Berry Swiers, and to my husband, Robert Beck.

Contents

Narrative Inquiry

1

An Introduction to Narrative Inquiry

A CALL FOR NARRATIVE IN SOCIAL WORK

Social work relies on relationships and on language-based strategies to promote functioning. Strategies include talk therapy, case management, education, advocacy, and supervision. As a result, language is central to the practice of social work. Whether the language is stories individuals tell in therapy, conversations between social work practitioners and clients, dialogue among members of a treatment or management team, exchanges between interviewers and research participants, or societal discourses upon which social workers and clients draw, language frames how individuals construct problems and their solutions—that is, action.

The language-based nature of social work is widely recognized. However, social work research has treated language spoken by practitioners, clients, and research participants as primarily signs of something else (see McLeod's [2001] critique of psychotherapy research for a similar point). For example, language is treated as a report of a symptom, an expression of a disorder, an endorsement or a rejection of an idea, or an elaboration of a concept. Researchers look "through language" *rather than* at language, for example, at the content of a story as it unfolds over time, its structure, the way in which it is performed, or how it is received and the cultural and other resources upon which it draws. Indeed, there is a limited amount of research within social work that focuses on language itself (Riessman & Speedy, 2007) (*see* the work of Hall and his colleagues [Hall, 1997; Hall, Slembrouch, & Sarangi, 2006] for notable exceptions). Perhaps this state of affairs is not surprising given the prevailing genre for scientific discourse emphasizes quantification (Chamberlain & Thompson, 1998).

Nonetheless, the primary assumption underlying this volume is that if social workers do not attend to language, we will be hobbled in our ability to understand others (and ourselves) and therefore our ability to restore or to enhance individuals' capacities to function socially or psychosocially, the core aim of the profession.

This volume is designed to promote study of language and, in particular, the study of narratives. It is addressed to doctoral students and researchers within and outside schools of social work for whom narrative inquiry is new. Drawing on theoretical and methodological papers written over the past 30 years within the social sciences and the humanities—that is, the human sciences (Hinchman & Hinchman, 1997)—and the professions (Charon, 2006; Clandinin, 2007; Delgado, 1988; Lieblich, McAdams, & Josselson, 2004; Mattingly & Garro, 2000; Montgomery, 1991), it provides an introduction to methods used to analyze narrative data.

The volume shows how these methods may be used to clarify phenomena of interest to social work, for example, to unearth a meaning of a seemingly incoherent story told by a woman suffering from schizophrenia (Gee, 1991); to show how family members, through family dinner-time conversations, shape each others' motivations to eat (Wiggins, Potter, & Wildsmith, 2001); to illustrate how working-class women construct addictive behavior, the societal discourses upon which they draw, and the implications of both for psychosocial interventions (Gillies, 1999); to examine how a sexually abusive young man sees himself, masculinity, others, and relationships (Emerson & Frosh, 2004); or to illustrate how a dialogue between a social worker and a mother evolves so that a mother's reason for wanting to relinquish her children is recast in relation to a "damaged identity" (Hall, Jokinen, & Suoninen, 2003).

WHAT IS NARRATIVE?

Narrative inquiry is a multidisciplinary enterprise that has moved beyond its origins in literature to include a diverse range of fields including anthropology, economics, history, psychology, sociology, and socio-linguistics, representing what has been called "the narrative turn" in the human sciences (Riessman, 2008).[1]

Scholars vary with respect to the definition of narrative, and differences depend on disciplinary framework, theoretical orientation, topic of study, and methodological approach employed (Squire, Andrews, & Tamboukou, 2008). Moreover, how narrative is understood is culturally framed so that it is important to acknowledge at the outset that much current knowledge of narrative and, by extension, this volume depend on the Western tradition.

Narrative has been defined commonly in relation to events. The definitions provided by Gergen (2009) as well as Hinchman and Hinchman (1997) represent dominant themes. For example, Gergen (2009) identifies definitional criteria for narrative in the West as including stories that have a valued end-point; that include events relevant to that point; that incorporate events in a coherent order, typically in relation to a linear conception of time; and that provide a sense of explanation. Hinchman and Hinchman (1997) offer a preliminary definition designed to be "the lowest common denominator of all definitions, the features of narrative that most theorists presumably would regard as indispensable to the intelligibility of their topic" (p. xv). Echoing Gergen (2009), they suggest a narrative is a story of events, placed in sequential order, which conveys meaning to a particular audience.

Although a useful starting point, these definitions omit narratives of experience broadly defined. Understanding experiences such as chronic conditions, phases in life, or turning points is also critical to social work practice. In this respect, Squire's (2008) approach to narratives is germane. She defines narratives of experience in relation to a broad approach to narrative inquiry that presumes that narratives are "sequential and meaningful," relate to human experience, re-present experience, and "display transformation or change" (p. 42). She argues that narratives are a way in which individuals make sense of themselves and the world. On this latter point, she highlights the work of Bruner (1990), who emphasizes that stories constitute individuals' efforts to restore violations of normality. In his later work, Bruner (2004) emphasizes the ways in which "self-making stories" are guided from the inside and from the outside—by memory and by validation from others—and how they are shaped by storytelling genres within a culture. Freeman (2007) underscored this view when he advanced the position that although narratives issue from a self, the forces that propel them forward are others: It is relationships that move "the self to speak, and narrative is its native language" (p. 18).

Whether focused on events or experience, narratives may be found in written material such as clinical reports, in speech such as interviews, in electronic communication such as text messages, or in visual forms such as photo diaries or film (*see* Riessman [2008] for a discussion of visual narratives). In fact, the source of a narrative also has implications for its definition. For example, when narratives are spoken (as would be the case when individuals recount narratives as a part of research interviews), the time, the place, the occasion, the narrator, the audience, and the narrative are immediately intertwined (Chamberlain & Thompson, 1998). Thus, "oral genres have to be understood as 'purposeful social actions' (p. 10)" in a way that written narratives do not.

Indeed, narratives may be considered in relation to their co-construction between, for example, an interviewer and a research participant (Mishler, 1997) or a therapist and a client (Mattingly, 1998). They may be shaped by the audience to whom they are told—for example, a worker at a child abuse hotline (Hall, 1997). Or, they may be formed by wider societal discourses on which a narrator may draw—for example, discourses defining a culturally specific understanding of who qualifies as worthy of social or economic assistance (Arribas-Allyson & Walkerdine, 2008).

A transcribed narrative may also be defined as one type of text and compared to other types of texts. Wengraf (2001), for example, compares narratives or stories to *descriptions* ("the assertion that certain entities have certain properties, but in a timeless and non-historical way. No attempt is made at story-telling/narration"…), *arguments* ("the development of argument and theorizing and position-taking, usually from a present-time perspective"…), *reports* ("a form in which a sequence of events, experiences and action is recounted, but in a relatively experience-thin fashion"…), and *evaluations* ("the 'moral of the story'— of a thin report or a rich narrative") (pp. 243–244).

Thus, defining what does *not* count as a narrative is as important as defining what does. However, the distinction between narrative and non-narrative talk or text is not always easily drawn. Some narratives may be fragmentary, submerged and awaiting a receptive audience to emerge (Plummer, 1995), or present in the silences or spaces of the story that is told (Bruner, 1990). Nuanced forms of narrative analysis probe such complexity (Hollway & Jefferson, 2000; Rogers, 2007; Rosenthal, 1998); however, they will not be included in this volume.

This volume focuses on first-person oral narratives of events or of experience (past or present, future or imaginary) obtained for purposes of research. In recognition of the variability in definition of the term, *narrative*, I do not advance a definitive one. Rather, I highlight the definition associated with each approach to analysis of narratives I examine. However, I use the term, *narrative*, and the term, *story*, to mean the same thing throughout the text.

WHAT IS NARRATIVE ANALYSIS?

The dominant methods with which to analyze language within the social sciences are narrative analysis, conversation analysis, and discourse analysis. *Narrative analysis* takes stories as its primary source of data and examines the content, structure, performance, or context of such narratives considered as a whole. As a result, narrative analysis relies on extended accounts "that are treated analytically as units, rather than fragmented into thematic categories", as would be the case in content analysis or the constant comparative method (Riessman, 2008, p. 12).

Whereas content analysis (Krippendorff, 2004) is useful when the interest is in the type and number of independent themes observed in a text, and the constant comparative method is useful when increasingly abstract thematic categories are conceptualized for the purpose of grounded theory development (Glaser & Strauss, 1967), narrative analysis is useful when the interest is in how and why a story is constructed as it is, what it accomplishes, and how the audience affects what may be told (Riessman, 2008).

Conversation analysis (Silverman, 1998a, 1998b, 2001) takes naturally occurring conversation as its primary source of data, examines closely its paralinguistic and linguistic features, and focuses, in particular, on the organization of brief stretches of talk—for example, turn-taking in conversations—in order to conceptualize how individuals use categories to construct a "moral universe" (Silverman, 2004). It generally does not focus on material external to the conversation that is transcribed for analysis as text.

Discourse analysis is a family of approaches to talk and text that emphasizes its broad meaning or the cultural discourses upon which it draws (Willig, 2008a). Some analysts are interested in how individuals use words to construct their reality and to manage their stakes in conversation, whereas others are interested in how individuals draw on discourses that are widely available in society that shape what is possible for them to think and to feel (Willig, 2003). Thus, investigators are concerned with not only how individuals produce discourse but also how they are products of discourse (Edley, 2001).

"[D]ifferent traditions called 'discourse analysis' have emerged in different disciplinary environments. Often these traditions are structured by, and against, the basic issues of the parent discipline" (Hepburn & Potter, 2007, pp. 168–169). For example, within linguistics, discourse analysis has focused on how sentences combine to form discourse; in cognitive psychology it has focused on how mental schemas are used to make sense of narrative; within social psychology it has focused on how discourse constructs reality; and within post-structuralism it has focused on how discourse constitutes objects and subjects (Potter, 2004).

The lines among these three forms of analysis, however, are blurred: some scholars have employed concepts from conversation analysis and others concepts from discourse analysis in their analysis of narratives (De Fina, Schiffrin, & Bamberg, 2006a). As a result, although this volume focuses on *narrative analysis*, it also includes important conversation- and discourse-analytic concepts used in analysis of narratives.

There is a range of approaches to the analysis of narratives: moreover, how narrative is analyzed is intertwined with how it is defined (Gulich & Quasthoff, 1985). An approach may deal with a narrative's *content* (what a narrative says [semantics]), a narrative's *structure* (how a narrative is put together to convey meaning [syntax]), or *interactional context* (pragmatics) (Mishler, 1986a). In addition, new approaches to narrative analysis are emerging that focus on how narrative, its performance, and context are intertwined.

In this volume, I represent major approaches with respect to analysis of each of these, believing that for an introductory text, scope is more important than depth of coverage. Taken together, these approaches show that narratives may be analyzed systematically and produce meaningful findings. Some narratives may be examined with more than one approach. It perhaps goes without saying that the methodological strategies employed are inseparable from the aspects of meaning we are able to observe (Ochberg, 2003).

THE NARRATIVE TURN

Polkinghorne (1988) locates his interest in narrative in:

> an unresolved personal conflict between my work as an academic researcher on the one hand and as a practicing psychotherapist on the other...[noting] I have not found the findings of academic research of much help in my work as a clinician...[and in a] loss of faith in the ability of research in the human disciplines to deliver on their original promise of helping to solve human and social problems (p. ix).

Believing that research into human problems modeled on the natural sciences was inherently limited, he turned to the form of knowledge upon which psychotherapists rely, "narrative knowledge": Psychotherapists "are concerned with people's stories: they work with case histories and use narrative explanations to understand why the people they work with behave the way they do" (p. x).

Hinchman and Hinchman (1997) speculate that the resurgence of narrative inquiry is due to "a disenchantment with theories ... that portray the self as a mere 'point' acted upon by external forces (p. xiv)"; a rejection of presumptions that social scientific knowledge may be stated in terms of an "abstractly conceived 'subject' of knowledge"; and a failure of quantitative methodologies to reflect the complexity of social phenomena.

Squire and colleagues (Squire, Andrews, & Tamboukou, 2008) find the antecedents of narrative social research in two movements within academia: the incorporation of humanistic approaches to research within sociology and psychology as well as the evolution of poststructuralist, postmodern, and deconstructionist approaches to narrative within the humanities. The first movement advanced the use of "holistic, person-centered approaches" to research, such as biographies and life histories that relied on narratives, and the second advanced ideas of "narrative fluidity and contradiction," "unconscious as well as conscious meanings," and "power relations within which narratives become possible" (p. 3).

The tensions between these two movements raise the question as to the ground on which narrative analysis stands: Should it be based on the presumption that the human subject can be understood as a subject who has a singular "voice" or perspective on experience, or should it be based on the presumption that the human subject is positioned within conflicting societal discourses, is fragmented, and is conflicted (Frosh, 2007)? The former view suggests the narrative analyst could provide an interpretation that has a consistent shape and direction; the latter suggests there is "no external point from which the true story of the subject can be told (p. 639)." Thus, an analysis could, at best, acknowledge that some experiences remain outside language (Frosh, 2002) and that there are multiple ways in which any story may be told.

On the other hand, these quite different traditions converge in their emphasis on narratives as modes through which individuals resist prevailing ideologies (Andrews, Squire, & Tamboukou, 2008) (*see* Bamberg & Andrews [2004] for further discussion of this issue); indeed, their re-presentation as analyzed texts may provoke the empathy for their tellers that is required for a meaningful consideration of the definition of a just and moral world (Nussbaum, 1995).

Scholarly work in narrative, biography, life history, and identity blossomed together. Chamberlayne, Bornat, and Wengraf (2000), in their discussion of the "turn to biographical methods" in the social sciences, link the resurgence of biographical narrative methods to a wide range of developments within history, sociology, and psycho-analysis, including efforts to account for individual agency; to include life experiences of those at the margins of society; to incorporate knowledge of subjectivity into the social sciences and knowledge of history into sociology; to the "rediscovery" of culture in social policy and to debates as to the differences between historical and narrative truth in psycho-analysis, among other things—in short, to link micro- and macro-levels of analysis.

NARRATIVE AND SOCIAL WORK

Storytelling is central to recovery from many of life's afflictions. Van der Merwe and Gobodo-Madikizela (2008), writing in a South African context, show how recovery from trauma requires "organization of traumatic experience into a coherent narrative about the past" (p. 39).

Not surprisingly, therefore, narrative therapy is well-established within social work. In one approach (White, 2007; White & Epston, 1990), individuals tell stories about their problems, are helped to "re-author" or "re-story" their experience, and are therefore empowered to live more fully in relation to core values and commitments.

Narrative is flourishing in social work education, as well. For example, the journal, *Reflections: Narratives of Professional Helping*, publishes personal accounts of practitioners reflecting on their work as psychotherapists, group workers, community organizers, and policymakers with the aim of providing readers new perspectives on how change occurs.

Somewhat paradoxically, within the United States, narrative has played a less prominent role in contemporary social work research than in social work practice or education (Riessman & Quinney, 2005; Riessman & Speedy, 2007). Explanations for this gap include: the cross-disciplinary nature of narrative inquiry and the time it takes to develop expertise in the field; the complex ethical issues narrative work may raise and the difficulties casting this work within the framework of Institutional Review Board guidelines developed for medical research; and the limited training in such methods and the corresponding difficulties new social work scholars have in fielding narrative investigations and in conceptualizing the nature of their contribution (Riessman & Quinney, 2005).

However, narrative methods are highly relevant for social work research. Cast within a case study design of research, they have the benefits of this approach (Flyvberg, 2007); these benefits include providing context-dependent knowledge critical to the development of any field, critical cases with which to test theory, and atypical and other cases with which to develop hypotheses or to refine conceptualizations.

Within the substantive areas of concern to social work, narrative inquiry may be used to understand, by way of illustration, the nature of professional-client encounters; the tacit dimensions of practice;

and the categories of service such as foster care that tend to be reified in much research. Narrative inquiry may also be used to study aspects of development that may otherwise be overlooked; the relational experiences at the heart of clinical work (Josselson, Lieblich, & McAdams, 2007; Mitchell, 2007); and the ways in which individuals negotiate social exclusion (Rustin & Chamberlayne, 2002). In short, narrative inquiry provides knowledge needed to fulfill the mission of social work.

FOCUS AND ORGANIZATION OF THE TEXT

Despite the "narrative turn" in the human sciences, there are few commonly agreed upon debates within narrative inquiry or rules for framing investigations, obtaining and analyzing narrative data, or presenting narrative findings (Squire, Andrews, & Tamboukou, 2008). Squire and colleagues note that "clear accounts of how to analyse the data ... are rare" (p. 1). This results in part from the difficulty of conveying the wide variety of disciplinary frameworks, theoretical orientations, and conceptual processes relevant to narrative inquiry.

Nonetheless, relevant narrative analytic volumes, chapters, and papers exist (Andrews, Squire, & Tamboukou, 2008; Cortazzi, 2001; Gulich & Quasthoff, 1985; Hiles & Cermák, 2008; Hollway & Jefferson, 2000; Mishler, 1986b, 1995; Murray, 2003; Riessman, 2008), and widely-cited authors include Clandinin and Connelly (2000); Czarniawska (2004); Elliott (2005); Herman & Vervaeck (2001); Lieblich, Tuval-Mashiach, & Zilber, 1998; Riessman (1993); and Wortham (2001). Gubrium and Holstein (2009) identify the work of Lieblich and her colleagues and that of Riessman as particularly helpful to those seeking guidance with respect to analysis of narrative data.

However, some of the sources are highly theoretical, and none focus exclusively on social work-related phenomena, include discourse and conversation analytic concepts used in narrative analysis, or address emerging approaches to analysis of narratives.

I wrote this book to begin to fill this gap in the methodological literature. I also wrote the book to provide a counterweight against the unfortunate discomfort with knowledge generated outside experimental and quasi-experimental designs and procedures implicit in mainstream social work research, at least within the contemporary

North American context. (*See* Rosenwald [2003] for a similar point in relation to academic psychology.)

As an introduction to narrative study, it provides an orientation to its scope, themes, and analytic strategies, thereby providing sufficient information with which to implement or to adapt existing methodological approaches. This chapter is intended to provide an orientation to narrative study. Chapter 2 examines the case study design, a design well-suited for narrative research but not the only one that could be used, and issues related to its definition and implementation. Chapter 3 examines issues pertaining to data collection, recording, and transcription.

Chapters 4, 5, and 7 present approaches to the analysis of narrative data. Chapter 4 examines three approaches to the analysis of narrative content. Chapter 5 examines three approaches to the analysis of narrative structure. Chapter 6 presents two approaches to the analysis of discourse and provides the foundation for understanding the use of discursive concepts employed in narrative-analytic frameworks discussed in Chapter 7. Chapter 7 considers two emerging approaches to the analysis of narratives, approaches that emphasize how narratives, the contexts in which they are told, and the wider societal discourses on which they draw, are inter-related. Appendix 1 contains a chart summarizing approaches to the analysis of narratives.

The final chapter, Chapter 8, addresses how to consider ethical issues in narrative research, how to present findings, and how to cast validity. Appendix 2 contains an outline for a narrative research proposal. One component of narrative inquiry, the conduct of literature reviews, is omitted. I refer the reader to the work of Cooper (2009) and the work of Fink (2009) on this topic.

I describe each data-analytic approach I cover in relation to the same set of dimensions (definition of narrative, theoretical orientation, central question, major concepts, orientation to method, and use). For each approach, I also summarize an exemplary investigation and cite key references. Some approaches depend on precise methodological guidelines; others depend on the application of broad concepts or principles of analysis. I encourage the reader to review foundational papers and the illustrative empirical investigations identified in this volume to learn the craft of narrative analysis.

The approaches I include neither define the range of data-analytic possibilities nor dictate how each should be employed. Qualitative inquiry over the past several decades is replete with examples of investigators who have developed successfully new modes of inquiry (Glaser & Strauss, 1967) or adapted successfully existing ones (Gregg, 2006) in order to develop new knowledge. Following Josselson and Lieblich (2003), most would concur that in the end, it is thinking rather than procedure that advances knowledge.

2

One Design for Narrative Study

THE CASE STUDY DESIGN

Reports of narrative studies typically include detail regarding the narrator, the narrative, and its analysis. Less common is detail regarding the disciplinary or theoretical framework from which the narrative method was derived, the research design, or how data were collected. Indeed, rarely is there a report in which all elements of a research plan are articulated fully.[1]

This is due in part to the lack of agreement among scholars as to the importance of epistemological and methodological framing of investigations and to the creative possibilities offered by use of narrative analytic methods in disciplinary frameworks and problem areas far from those in which they originated. Nonetheless, scholarship is advanced by an effort to consider all of the traditional elements of a research plan for narrative inquiry and to consider the extent to which they fit together logically.

Toward that end, in this chapter, I present a research design in which much narrative study may be framed, the case study design (Stoecker, 1991), but I note that it is not the only one. Riessman (2008), for example, observes that narrative data-analytic methods may be employed usefully within a wide range of research designs. Padgett (2008) discusses ways in which qualitative and quantitative research methods may be mixed and the challenges posed by such efforts.

DEFINITION OF THE CASE STUDY

The case study design is characterized by a focus on a *case*, variously defined, rather than by a focus on a specific unit, type of data, or method of data collection or analysis (Willig, 2008b). The case may be an individual, a couple, a family, or a group of social-psychological interest, although the term, *case*, has also been defined as a type of experience (Willig, 2008b) or, less commonly, as a theoretical construct (Ragin, 1992).

Case studies have a long tradition in social work research (Gilgun, 1994), and, in fact, the term originated with the use of case or life histories written by social workers in "key books of the case study tradition" (Platt, 1992). However, the term, *case study*, should be distinguished from the term, *case history* (detailed clinical reports of individuals), and the term, *casework* (individually oriented social work).

Purposes

Although the purposes of case studies have been cast in several ways (*see* Willig [2008b] for one typology), the approach of McAdams and West (1997), writing in relation to personality psychology, is especially straightforward. They propose the primary functions of case studies as *exemplification* (the use of a case to illustrate theoretical concepts); *discovery* (the use of a case to conceptualize concepts or to develop hypotheses); and *comparison* (to compare critically one or more cases to a theory or to compare theories through study of one or more cases.) They argue further that the strongest case studies are those of the comparative type, especially those that involve multiple theories and methods; however, a study's contribution depends on the state of knowledge of the phenomenon under study at the time it is conducted.

Defining Features

Despite the diversity of purpose and approach, case studies have a number of features in common, including an "idiographic perspective," "attention to contextual data," incorporation of "a temporal element," and a concern "with theory" (Willig, 2008b). Thus, the case study design allows for an intensive examination of a phenomenon in context.

A case study, therefore, should not be confused with the "one-shot case study," in that it does not rely on a single measurement after completion of a treatment, or with the "single-subject research design," an experimental design for the study of the effects of a stimulus on behavior (McAdams & West, 1997).

SIGNIFICANCE OF CASE STUDIES

The purposes of case studies point to their significance for knowledge development. For example, case studies may provide the detailed knowledge necessary for the advancement of professional practice (Flyvberg, 2007). McAdams and West (1997) describe, for example, how Freud used case studies to exemplify psycho-analytic concepts. Flyvberg argues, moreover, that the "*force of example* has been under-estimated" in the evolution of social scientific knowledge.

Case studies may be used to formulate hypotheses, and one method, analytic induction (Robinson, 1951; Patton, 2002), has been developed to do so relying on the case study design (*see* Gilgun [1995] for an example of such in the social work literature).²

Case studies may also be used to falsify existing theory—that is, one may be able to identify, through intensive study of one case, instances of a phenomenon that should but do not confirm existing theory (Campbell, 1975; Flyvberg, 2007; Gobo, 2007)—or to test hypotheses. The findings from such work may be generalized to relevant theory (*see* Yin [2003] for a discussion of theoretical or analytic generalization).³

Some have even argued that when the phenomenon under study is expected or known to be homogenous, findings from a representative case may be generalized to a larger population (Gobo, 2007).

Alternatively, others have asserted that context-free propositions are not possible for social science and, by extension, case study research. Building on the work of Cronbach (1975), who argued the social world is too unstable for findings from social science research to be generalized, Lincoln and Guba (1985) believe that when proper recognition is given to the uniqueness of each phenomenon that has been studied, any finding is a working hypothesis.

CASE STUDIES AND NARRATIVE INQUIRY

In the late 1990s, McAdams and West (1997) pointed to a resurgence of case studies that employed narrative methods to examine subjective experience. Wengraf (2001) elaborated the potential of such work, arguing that biographical narratives allow investigators to connect subjective experience to social context because they inevitably contain the embedded assumptions and patterns of reasoning that characterize the narrator's society. Roberts (2002), writing in relation to biographical research, specified the point, showing how narratively informed life history research is ideal for study of personal transformations of all kinds, including those of keen interest to social work such as how individuals, groups, and communities recover from adverse events or upheavals in the social or natural environment.[4]

The investigations I highlight in this volume fall within the broad category of narrative case studies, though they may not have been framed originally as such. For example, through a close examination of two cases, contemporary and ancient warriors, and relying on narrative data, Shay (1994) developed a social-psychological explanation of post-traumatic stress disorder among veterans who experienced long-term combat.

DEFINITION OF THE CASE

Definition of the case, or the focus of study, differs from and is logically prior to the identification and selection of sources of information for the study (Ragin, 1992; Stake, 2000). Prior to the conduct of a case study, investigators should elucidate criteria for selection of the case to be examined.

For example, Squire (2007a) was interested in how South Africans were finding ways to "live with, speak about, and resist HIV." Thus, in her investigation the case was contemporary South Africans living within an HIV epidemic. (However, she might have cast the case more narrowly in terms of contemporary South Africans infected with HIV, or she might have cast the case more broadly in terms of individuals facing epidemics in the developing world. Addressing the question—What is the case?—is not as simple as it might first appear [Ragin & Becker, 1992].)

SELECTION OF THE SAMPLE

Identification of sources of information for a case study follows the logic of purposeful sampling rather than the more familiar logic of probability sampling. In probability sampling, a sample that represents the population is drawn to allow generalization of study findings to the population. In purposeful sampling, by way of contrast, sources of information are selected because they are expected to yield in-depth information with which to achieve the study's aim (Patton, 2002). Prior to the conduct of the case study, the investigator should elucidate criteria for selection of research participants.

For example, in Squire's study, although the case was contemporary South Africans living within an HIV epidemic, the sample was 37 individual South Africans near Cape Town.

It is important to note, however, that the sample may refer to units other than people such as narratives within a long interview or types of conversations (Willig, 2008b).

Purposeful Sampling Strategies

The investigator's sampling strategy depends ultimately on the study's aim. For example, investigators wishing to exemplify a concept or theoretical understanding might recruit research participants believed to be typical of the phenomenon of interest. Alternatively, investigators wishing to discover hypotheses or to develop explanations might recruit research participants who meet a criterion or who represent a theoretical construct. Patton (2002) presents a detailed list of purposeful sampling strategies for use in qualitative studies of all types.

For example, Squire employed a criterion-based sampling strategy. She recruited research participants who were highly motivated to speak about their experiences with HIV through nongovernmental organizations that provided HIV treatment.

Number of Participants

Sampling inevitably raises the question as to the number of participants to include as sources of information. The number selected should relate to the study's purpose, the extensiveness of the data-collection effort (e.g., how participants are interviewed, the questions they are asked, and the number of times they are interviewed), the richness of the data obtained vis-à-vis the study's purpose, and the thoughtfulness with which the study findings are linked to theoretical, empirical, and clinical literatures.

For example, studies designed to exemplify theoretical concepts may require only one research participant; studies designed to formulate hypotheses or to refine concepts may require many more, whereas comparative studies designed to test hypotheses or theories may require only a few.

In case studies employing narrative methods, however, the number of research participants required also varies in relation to the intensity of the analysis of language to be undertaken. Projects involving highly detailed analyses require fewer participants than those involving less-detailed approaches. The number, five, is sufficient for most studies involving complex analyses. Indeed, many widely cited narrative papers—particularly those designed to illustrate a method of narrative analysis—involve an *n* of one (*see*, for example, Gee, 1991).

ILLUSTRATION

Bar-On's research (1991) shows how one investigator moved—albeit with some distress—from a quasi-experimental design to a narrative case study. His initial interest was how descendents of perpetrators of the Holocaust in World War II coped with knowledge of their parents' terrible deeds. Initially operating within the logic of probability sampling, he intended to compare and contrast the children of perpetrators with the children of non-perpetrators, or "children of war." However, the rationale for the plan weakened, as he reviewed the interview data he had collected and found the variability within and across groups too great to sustain a comparison or even to interpret. Moreover, he came to believe that the lack of knowledge about the population doomed claims of representativeness to failure.

He gradually abandoned the logic of probability sampling and turned toward a different approach to sampling and to method writ large. Although he described the evolving approach in somewhat different language, in effect, he began to focus on children of perpetrators (the case);

he selected participants to study on the basis of the relevance of the information that each might provide to the study's questions (purposeful sampling); and he began to develop theoretical concepts with which to understand the data he had collected, thereby redirecting his study's purpose to theoretical development or discovery. Eventually, relying on narrative and other types of data, he conceptualized a process through which children of perpetrators "worked through" their childhood experiences, and he wrote a book in which research participants' interviews were included so that readers could derive their own conclusions as to significance of his analysis.

EVALUATION OF CASE STUDIES

An evaluation of the utility of a case study depends ultimately on its primary purpose. However, scholars concerned with how to evaluate the validity of case studies of all types argue they should contain the following elements: a clear purpose; a restricted focus; a specification of what constitutes the case and a consideration of the boundary between the case and its context; a delineation of the methods used to examine the question upon which the case study focuses; a separation of data and interpretations of data; an evaluation of alternative explanations for the data; and a statement as to the limitations of the conclusions drawn (Willig, 2008b).

In the end, the trustworthiness of the case study will hinge, however, on the quality of the logic linking study purpose, data, and conclusions (*see* Runyan, 1980, for a useful discussion of an older literature than I have included in this chapter on this topic). Approaches to the evaluation of studies, including case studies, that depend on narrative are delineated in Chapter 8 of this volume.

CONCLUSION

This chapter has defined the purposes of case study research, located narrative inquiry in relation to the case study design, and suggested ways in which the investigator may define a case, select a sample, identify an appropriate number of subjects (or units) from which to obtain narrative data, and evaluate the trustworthiness of case studies. As such, it provides a framework in which the various strategies of collection and analysis of narrative data (to which I turn in succeeding chapters) may be placed.

3

Framework for Collection of Narrative Data

S tories are told by someone, to someone else, at one or more points in time, and in a specific historical and cultural context. The individual to whom a story is told, whether the individual is a research interviewer or another, may shape the story that emerges. Undoubtedly, a story, its construction and performance, and the circumstances under which it is told are reflexively inter-related (Gubrium & Holstein, 2009).

Any one method of narrative analysis does not and probably cannot address this complexity in its totality, and, in fact, none of the data-analytic approaches to analysis of narratives covered in this volume attempts to do so. Indeed, some narrative analytic methods emerge from disciplinary traditions with their own theoretical assumptions as to the importance of narrative construction, performance, and environment in tow.

To provide the broadest possible framework in which to consider collection of data for narrative inquiry, however, this chapter suggests the kinds of data that could be collected for a range of approaches to the analysis of narratives. Thus, the chapter covers not only how to collect narratives but also the questions one might ask and the concepts and strategies one might employ in order to understand how narratives are co-constructed, performed, and shaped by the sites in which they are produced. This framework depends on the work of Gubrium and Holstein (2009), who have advanced an ethnographically informed approach to the analysis of narratives, as delineated in their recent volume, *Analyzing Narrative Reality*. At the conclusion of the chapter, I consider how to audio-record and to transcribe narratives.

COLLECTION OF NARRATIVES

Qualitative Interview Formats

Although narratives may be contained in printed material or constructed from visual material, this volume focuses on oral narratives produced within the context of qualitative research interviews. Qualitative interviews may be designed so that they encourage development of narratives, although it is important to note that narratives may also emerge spontaneously in the context of data- collection activities of all types, including highly structured interviews designed to yield quantitative data.

Patton (2002) identifies three types of qualitative interviews— "the informal conversational interview," the "general interview guide approach," and the "standardized open-ended interview." The informal conversational interview is one in which the interviewer, although guided by the purpose of the study, asks questions in the course of a naturally occurring conversation of the sort that occurs in ethnographic fieldwork (Spradley, 1979); the general interview guide approach is one in which the interviewer asks questions in relation to a predetermined set of topics; and the standardized open-ended interview is one in which the interviewer asks specific questions in a prescribed order.

Framing Interview Questions

All three types of qualitative interviews depend, however, on what Patton refers to as a "truly open-ended" question—that is, a question that allows the interviewee to respond to the question in his or her own words, as would be the case in a question such as Could you please tell me about how you came to leave your country? This question stands in contrast to a question in which the categories of response are implied or are specified in advance, as would be the case in a question such as, Could you please tell me about the difficulties you experienced in relation to leaving your country? or Could you please rate how difficult it was to leave your country on a scale from 1 to 5, with 1 being "not at all difficult" and 5 being "very difficult"?

Investigators might also ask directly for stories, as would be the case in questions such as, Could you tell me the story of what happened when the caseworker came to remove your child from your home? or in questions such as, Could you tell me the story of your life, starting wherever you would like to begin? (Kvale, 2007).

Interview texts (Kvale, 2007; Wengraf, 2001) stress the importance of posing open-ended questions that are clear, contain one idea, are devoid of academic language; that emphasize what or *how* something was experienced rather than *why* something occurred; and that yield detailed descriptions of concrete experience (Patton, 2002).

Interview vs. Research Questions

The ability to cast such questions is supported by an understanding of at least two distinctions: The first distinction is between a study's primary research question, a question such as, How do sexually-abusive boys make sense of their sexually-abusive behavior? and the interview questions asked of such a boy, such as What would you say you've learned about being a boy/by growing up in your home? (Emerson & Frosh, 2004). The second is the distinction between an interviewer's stance toward the interviewee as a person and an interviewer's stance toward what the interviewee has to say. On this point, Patton (2002) argues the interviewer should respect and perhaps empathize with the interviewee but should convey a nonjudgmental attitude toward the content of the interviewee's speech. Some projects have floundered over the investigator–interviewer's failure to maintain these distinctions (Kvale, 2007; Wengraf, 2001).

Most of the narrative analytic frameworks discussed in this volume are paired with specific open-ended interview questions, and these questions are noted in the section devoted to the discussion of each framework covered. Thus, understanding how to frame a narrative-pointing interview question will be furthered by considering: *What type of interview question has been employed in the narrative data-analytic method selected for the investigation, and does this form suit the purpose of the investigation at hand?*

Linking Questions and Responses

Narratives are linked inevitably to the questions that prompt them, although narrative analytic frameworks vary in the extent to which this link is emphasized. Gubrium and Holstein (2009), drawing on work in conversation analysis (Sacks, Schegloff, & Jefferson, 1974; Silverman, 1998a; Silverman, 1998b), suggest one way in which this connection may be conceptualized. They argue that a narrative may be considered as one type of "turn" at talk, even when that talk is prompted by an interviewer. To illustrate this point, Gubrium and Holstein (2009) ask readers to consider the implications for responses of the questions below, each of which is designed to obtain life history data (*see* p. 46):

> "Why don't you tell me about your life?"
>
> "A lot of people think of their lives as having a particular course, as having gone up and down. Some people think it hasn't gone down. Some people see it as having gone in a circle. How do you see your life?"
>
> "As you look back over your life, what are some of the milestones that stand out?"
>
> "Let me ask you this. If you were writing a story of your life, what chapters would you have in your book? Like what would the first chapter be about?"

Thus, the narratives elicited by the questions above would vary in relation to the form and content of the questions that preceded them. Thus, understanding a narrative will be furthered by the collection of data relevant to understanding the question: *How might a narrative and the questions that preceded it be linked?*

Sustaining Narrative Production

Interview questions that launch a narrative could be supported by a process that Kvale (2007) refers to "active listening," or the art of posing follow-up questions in a way that invites the interviewee to deepen and to expand the story being told. However, narrative analytic methods vary widely in the extent to which interviewers are encouraged to do so (*see* Rosenthal [1993, 1998] and Wengraf [2001] for descriptions of a method that requires interviewers to remain as uninvolved as possible in the first of the two life history interviews that are conducted in the biographic-narrative method). Thus, elicitation and elaboration of narratives may be furthered by addressing the question: *How and on what theoretical grounds should the interviewer engage with the interviewee?*

For example, interviewing strategies tend to vary in relation to how narrative is defined (Squire, 2008): Those who treat a narrative as being within the person tend to ask a few relatively straightforward questions to elicit and to sustain narrative production; those who treat narrative as a joint product of the exchange between an interviewer and an interviewee tend to engage in a more active interviewing style; and those who treat narrative as having objective and subjective components tend to ask specific questions about an interviewee's life history (the facts) and open-ended questions about an interviewee's life story (how the facts are constructed as a story).

Co-Construction of Narratives

Narratives may be considered not only in relation to the specific questions that prompt or sustain them but also in relation to the entire interaction between an interviewer and interviewee. Although specific narrative analytic frameworks vary with respect to whether or not co-construction is considered an analytic issue, an emerging consensus among qualitative methodologists is that an interview is a joint accomplishment of the interviewer and interviewee (Fontana & Prokos, 2007). Even in situations in which an investigator/interviewer attempts to minimize his or her role, the interviewer helps to shape the interviewee's talk through not only the way in which questions are asked but also the way in which responses are acknowledged both verbally and nonverbally in relation to, for example, pitch or volume of voice, pacing of speech, body movements, or use of interpersonal space.

Considering narratives, however, as co-constructed does not necessarily mean that interviewers and interviewees share the same view (Capps & Ochs, 1995) but rather that storytelling is responsive to the individual perspectives of the interviewer and interviewee, their interactions, as well as their social locations. In this view, interviews are sites of knowledge production, and the form this knowledge takes is linguistic (Kvale, 2007). Thus, understanding how a story is told will be furthered by the collection of data relevant to the analysis of the question *How do those involved in storytelling relate to each other in narrative production?*

Control Over Narratives

Co-construction of a narrative raises the question of ownership—especially in storytelling situations in which there is competition for narrative control. Efforts to control narrative may be formal, such as making a claim to direct knowledge of an event under discussion, or they may be informal, such as one dialogic partner discounting the language of another in accordance with discourse rules embedded in a specific institutional context.

Hall and his colleagues provide a useful illustration of narrative co-construction and control in their study of negotiations between social workers and mothers relinquishing custody of their children (Hall, Jokinen, & Suoninen, 2003, p. 4). In this study, the focus is on how a mother and a social worker reach agreement that relinquishment should occur within the context of the dialogue between the two.

In the stretch of talk between a social worker (labeled SW) and a mother (labeled M) reported in Box 3–1, one can see how the dialogue

---

Box 3–1

1. SW: hhhwhy do you think thathh it is better for the children that they go
2.   and live with their father.
3.   (3)
4. M: Well see, (.) we have sort of, (.) problems, (.) in the family,
5.   (1.5)
6. SW: With whom.
7.   (1.5)
8. M: Ah well see, (1). . . . (1.5) the problem is kind ofhhhh me and, (.) my current
9.   husband.
10.   (4)
11. SW: hhhh krh rhh ((coughs)) your husband . . .(.) gets along, (.) with your children
12.   from your prev-,(.) previous marriage, (.) or, (.) how do you mean.
13. M: No he gets along with them all right. (.) But I can't cope.
14. SW: Well ho-h__ow does the
15.   problem come about.
16. M: I can't cope with this, (.) circus.
17.   (1.7)
18. SW: So who do y__ou not get along with.
19. M: Well, (.) children and (1.5) this, (.) combination,
20.   (1) husband and, (.) children
21.   (1.5)

(Continued)

Box 3–1 (*Continued*)

22. SW: Husband and children.
23. M: Mm.
24. SW: hhh Then what kind of hhh, (.) problems,(.) do you h<u>a</u>ve, in your home
25.   situation, (.) family situation.
26.   (1.5)
27. M: Well mainly sort of mental health problems.
28.   (2)
29. M: I have a mental health problems, and (.) then well, mthh, (.) my husband has
30.   this <u>a</u>lcohol problem (.) and I think that's two good reasons for, (4) for well,
31.   (.) me being h<u>e</u>re now (.)
32. SW: Mm.
33. M: Mm.
34. SW: mthh So you feel that you cannot take c<u>a</u>re of the children.
35. M: Yes. (.)
36. SW: Yes. (1.5) hh That you haven't got the str<u>e</u>ngth to see to their basic, (.)
37. M: No
38. SW: Basic needs and things (.). yes.

Source: Hall, C., Jokinen, A., & Suoninen, E. (2003). Legitimating the rejecting of your child in a social work meeting. In C. Hall (Ed.), *Constructing clienthood in social work and human services: Interaction, identities, and practices* (pp. 27–43). London: Jessica Kingsley.

---

evolves so that a mother's reason for wanting to relinquish her children is recast in relation to a "damaged identity." In this text, a dot enclosed in parentheses (.) indicates a pause of less than two-tenths of a second; parentheses that enclose a number reflect the length of the pause in tenths of a second; and a letter or word that is underlined refers to a sound that was emphasized in speech.

This stretch of talk shows how a story of why the children in the family must be removed from the parents' care is slowly being co-constructed in the dialogue between the social worker and the mother and that a struggle over control of the narrative is in play. For example, the mother advances early in the exchange a general reason, that of "problems in the family", for removal. The worker attempts to specify the nature of the problems, an attempt the mother resists.

The mother then reluctantly specifies, as reflected in the number and length of pauses in her speech, the problems in terms of her "mental health problems," and her husband's "alcoholism." The social worker then explicitly links these problems to the mother's inability to care for her children. The social worker moves to question the husband and then the mother again, asking if the husband is violent, which the mother confirms.

In short, "[h]er opening position that it was her decision of what is best has been ignored in the requirement to produce a damaged identity of an abused woman living with a violent and alcoholic husband. In these circumstances, it is not only legitimate to give up her children, but also probably in the children's best interests (p. 35)."

Hall and his colleagues note that co-constructed stories such as the one noted above share a resemblance to Garfinkel's conceptualization of degradation ceremonies and to Foucault's conceptualization of confession and ask why social workers reformulate "mothers' identities in disparaging terms before agreement and a way forward is established (p. 42)," thereby raising fundamental questions regarding the nature of child welfare practice.

Creating Space for Narratives

Investigators in research interviews typically work hard to create a space in which interviewees have control of the stories that they tell. However, this is not a straightforward task (Hydén, 2008). Hydén discusses strategies that facilitate such control, including conducting interviews in physical spaces that are conducive to storytelling, pursuing topics in a way that does not presume the prevailing discourse on the topic, and opening discursive space by challenging a narrative performance or redirecting the course of the interview.

The text in Box 3–2, drawn from a transcript of Hydén's interview with an abusive man (Hydén, 1995, p. 58), provides a compelling example of the latter strategy. In this text, IP refers to the abusive man, and H refers to Hydén. Hydén (2008) notes that his story is similar to the stories of other men who have beaten their wives, and the basic storyline was something like this: "My wife has been beaten (severely in most cases) and I am very sorry, but I cannot be held responsible because . . . (p. 132)."

Box 3–2

IP: you see, in our heads there is a place with two poles. There has to be a certain distance between them. When you get angry, you get close to one of the poles. In my head, the poles are too close together, so that when I get angry, they crash into each other. I can see on your face that you don't believe me, but it is in fact true. A doctor himself told me this. I think it was caused by a motorcycle accident I was in.

M: How can you tell when this happens?

IP: I simply have a total blackout. I get mad and then BANG, it crashes and I am Not aware of anything for a long time. When I come to again, I have often done something violent. Hit Pia (his wife) or trashed the apartment.

Then I posed the question that made his story follow another direction:

M: Then it must be unbelievable luck that Pia is still alive.

IP: What do you mean?

H: I mean that when you get mad at her and it short-circuits in your head, your body takes on a life of its own and becomes violent. It's lucky that you haven't stuck the bread knife in her, or scissors, or hit her even worse than you have.

IP: Are you crazy or something??!! Do you really think I could do such a thing? I would never hurt her that bad.

Source: Hydén, M. (2008). Narrating sensitive topics. In M. Andrews, C. Squire, & M. Tamboukou (Eds.), *Doing narrative research* (pp. 121–136). Los Angeles, CA: Sage.

By challenging her interviewee's oft-repeated narrative, Hydén created a space in which other more detailed and complex stories of abuse could emerge.

Thus, understanding how a story is told will be furthered by the examination of the analytic question: *During turn-taking exchanges, which stories are advanced and how?*

SUPPRESSION OF NARRATIVES

Indeed, narratives that are advanced and those that are absent may overlap in complex ways, with traces of the suppressed narrative present in the provided one. Gubrium and Holstein (2009) urge narrative analysts to consider how entitlement to tell a story is demonstrated in a narrative in order to understand narrative activation and silencing in its broadest context. Shuman (2005) provides detail as to the conditions that make stories tellable or untellable in a particular social historical context. She argues that the former relies on socially-accepted categories and the latter on unrecognizable or socially unacceptable categories. She provides an example of an unrecognizable narrative, when she quotes Edward Said's response to the "charge that the Palestinians needed better narratives" (Shuman, p. 19):

> The narratives have been there. They're of a different sort . . . it's essentially not a Western narrative. The model of wandering and exile is available. I. F. Stone always says the Palestinians have become the "Jews of the Middle East." But that's a borrowed narrative . . . [. . . in the original]. After all, this [the Palestinian narrative] is a narrative that always has to compete with a very powerful, already existent narrative of resurgent nationalism of the retributive kind, of the sort that one associates with Zionism. So on a lot of fronts there are formal problems (Said, 1990, p. 138).

Shuman (2005) concludes that the legitimacy of a narrative depends ultimately on perceptions of the entitlement of the narrator to narrate, whether the story form helps the experience to which it refers to be understood, and on the web of "interpersonal and intertextual relationships in which the story and the experience are entwined (p. 24)."

However, suppressed stories may evolve into *counter-narratives* that resist and undermine dominant narratives (Bamberg & Andrews, 2004; Delgado, 1988) through an interactional process that transforms both. When narratives are in conflict, individuals may work to negate or de-legitimize the story to which they are opposed (Bar-On, 2006).

Plummer (1995) specifies and advances the point when he notes that stories become not only tellable but also widely available, when there is an audience to listen to the story and when others amplify and make space for the story in a given cultural context. For example, after studying the widespread distribution of sexual stories in the 1960s and 1970s, he concluded:

> Stories whose time has come will be those that have entered this culture of public problems, the political spectacle. With this, there will be (1) a large number of people willing to claim it as their own, (2) a willingness to tell the story very visibly so that others can identify with it and (3) the

presence of allies who do not claim the story as their own, but who are keen to give it credibility and support (p. 129).

In sync with Gubrium and Holstein (2009), Shuman (2005) places narrative in the context of ethnography and argues that in order to understand whether narratives remain private or move into a public domain, the investigator might collect data relevant to questions such as, *Whose story is it? What is it being used for? What does it promise and at whose expense?*

PERFORMANCE OF NARRATIVES

Although narrative co-construction and control focuses on the conversational interactions that shape a story, the concept, *narrative performance,* focuses on the broad way in which a story is told. Langellier (1989) distinguishes between aspects of storytelling that enhance the experience of telling or listening to a story, aspects such as providing vivid detail or the use of gestures, and the ways in which storytelling shapes or even destabilizes the identities of storyteller and audience. Gubrium and Holstein (2009) emphasize that stories are staged—that is, they are told to someone for specific purposes. Goffman (1959) uses the concept of performance to conceptualize ways in which social actors perform preferred identities, especially in situations in which they wish to save face.

Riessman (2008) highlights Langellier's (2001) analysis of five stories told by a cancer survivor. It illustrates the complex inter-relationships between a story, its performance, and identity. The narrator in Langellier's study, a woman who had suffered from breast cancer, a mastectomy, and had the mastectomy scar tattooed, sought to "redefine self and tattoo by strategically navigating the contradictory meanings of her multiply marked body (p. 149)." Langellier shows how the language that the narrator uses to tell the stories reflects the evolution of the meaning of her identity over time. Langellier cautions, however, that the woman's narrative performance engages

as much with social arrangements as with self-conceptions; the tattooed body is the performative boundary between inner and outer, self and world. At the social level the reformulation of possibilities for self takes

the form of critique of the very categories by which society defines the
stigma and deviance of breast cancer, mastectomy, and tattoo . . . [her]
tattoo narrative constitutes not only a personal transformation but also
a social and political story of transgression (p. 171).

Thus, this work serves as a hedge against essentializing notions of not
only self but also of survivorship.

Gubrium and Holstein (2009) argue for the importance of tracing
how speakers produce effects and how listeners respond to what is
said. Thus, understanding how a story is told will be furthered by the
collection of data relevant to addressing the questions: *Who is the audience for the story? How is narrative performed? What are the expectations
and responses of the audience? How do the narrator and audience work to
shape the story that is told?*

COLLECTION OF NARRATIVE-RELATED DATA

In addition to the collection of data pertaining to narratives and the
interactional context in which they are constructed and performed, narratives may also be affected by the broader environment in which they
are told. Gubrium and Holstein (2009) refer to this environment as the
"narrative environment." Within this category they include the contexts
such as families and occupations, the cultures of which they are a part,
and the other discourses of which narratives may be a part. I highlight
two of these as especially relevant to narrative inquiry in the context of
social work practice here.

Professions as Sites for Narratives

Professional practice is an important environment in which narratives
are produced. Individuals in a profession share the same type of training,
skills, values, and perspectives, and often they operate within shared
professional or legal frameworks. As a result, practitioners typically use
"specialized vocabulary to convey precise, job-specific actions that are
especially germane to the collective work of the group concerned
(Gubrium & Holstein, 2009, p. 163)."

Scholars have used narrative methods to study the practice of law (Delgado, 1988), medicine (Charon, 2006), psychotherapy (Lieblich, McAdams, & Josselson, 2004), and occupational therapy (Mattingly, 1998), among others.

Gubrium and Holstein (2009) highlight an illuminating example of professional narratives at work in the text reproduced in Box 3–3. The text is drawn from a study by Holstein (1988, pp. 272–273) in which he examines a transcript of two professionals, a judge (labeled J.) and a therapist (labeled T.), discussing a patient at an involuntary commitment hearing.

What emerges from an examination of the transcript is that the two professionals view the case quite differently and in relation to their professional orientations: For the therapist, the family is defined broadly and in relation to the patient's treatment; whereas for the judge, the family is defined conventionally and in relation to the patient's need for control and the community's need for protection. Therefore, Gubrium and Holstein (2009) emphasize the methodological importance of obtaining

---

Box 3–3

J: Where's Mr. Biggs gonna stay while he's being treated?

T: Tyrone lives with his family. They have an apartment in Lawndale.

J: I thought Mr. Biggs was divorced last year?

T: He was, your honor. But he's moved in with his girlfriend and their two children. They share a place with her aunt. He really seems to be getting along fine.

J: Now who is it that takes care of him? You say these two ladies are going to be able to keep him out of trouble. How long has he lived with them? What happens when he gets delusional again?

T: We're hoping that's under control. . . . I think it's important to understand that being close to his family is extremely important to Tyrone's [treatment] program. His family wants him there and they make him feel like he belongs. He needs that kind of security—the family environment—it he's ever going to learn to cope and he's not going to get it from anyone but his family.

J: That may be so, but you still haven't told me who will keep him under control. Who's going to make him take his medication? . . . I just don't see any family there to look out for him. . .

Source: Gubrium, J. & Holstein, J. (2009). *Analyzing narrative reality.* Los Angeles, CA: Sage.

ethnographic data pertaining to individuals at work in order to identify the work-related issues that shape narratives.

Hall and Slembrouck (in press) identify what some of those issues might be within the context of child welfare practice: They emphasize the importance of understanding how, through dialogue, parents and social workers construct what is good or bad, justifiable or unjustifiable, or acceptable or unacceptable. Thus, understanding a narrative will be furthered by collection of data relevant to addressing these questions: *How are formal categories of a profession used to "certify" or "authorize" the narratives to which they are related?*

Local Culture

Gubrium and Holstein (2009) are particularly interested in how the "big stories" of various settings are reflexively related to the "little stories" of individuals within those settings. They emphasize the importance of examining how individuals construct in narrative "who and what they are, especially as this varies in time and social place (p. 137)" in order to make the connection.

They highlight the work of ethnographer Anderson (1999) to illustrate the importance of understanding the local culture in which narratives are produced. Relying on ethnographic data pertaining to young people's sexual relationships and narrative data pertaining to young people's stories of their sexual experiences that he obtained through intensive field work in an African-American community, Anderson shows how one young woman's story of a date may be read as a "seduction plot," as the first step toward the realization of a dream of a family and a home, or perhaps as both, revealing an ambiguity of meaning that would not be evident if the narrative text were analyzed alone.

Thus, understanding a story and its telling will be furthered by the collection of data pertaining to the question: *What is the local context in which this story must be understood?*

Beyond Local Context

Context does not have to be considered primarily in relation to a small geographical or to a specific cultural space, however. Phoenix (2008) shows how narratives of personal experience draw on canonical narratives and reference wider societal contexts.[1] For example, Squire (2007a) describes how the HIV-affected South African subjects in her study told their stories not only to her but also to those who would listen to the audio-recordings of the interviews, those who would read the study reports, and those involved in the wider South African and global discourse concerned with HIV/AIDS.

Summary

In summary, although the analysis of a narrative may focus exclusively on one aspect of, for example, its content, structure, or performance, this portion of the chapter shows how any analysis might be deepened by a close examination as to how narratives are suppressed, collected, and sustained; co-constructed and controlled; and affected by the institutional and other discursive contexts of which they are a part.

Investigators should evaluate critically, however, the field notes they take in order to study these contexts: The ways in which others are represented in field notes and the rhetorical strategies used to warrant claims made are linked inevitably to study findings (Wolf, 1992).

RECORDING AND TRANSCRIBING NARRATIVES

The information required to examine the analytic questions posed in this chapter requires extensive reading on the topic under study, observations and related field notes pertaining to the circumstances under which a narrative is told, and detailed transcriptions of audio-recorded oral interviews. Several volumes consider how to collect field notes (Emerson, Fretz, & Shaw, 1995; Lofland & Lofland, 1995; Padgett, 2008). Here I turn my attention to a relatively neglected area of research practice—that is, how to re-present audio-recordings of research interviews as text (Mishler, 1991). The procedure used to do so is referred to as *transcription*. Transcription is central to the narrative analytic frameworks included in this volume.

The older view that summarizing or paraphrasing a narrator's words is adequate for narrative research has been abandoned. Inclusion of all of the narrator's words—that is, the production of a verbatim transcription—is considered crucial to a full analysis of his or her story. This means that ungrammatical or colloquial speech is not "tidied up" to make it sound better (Poland, 2002).

Transcription As Interpretation

However, transcription is not simply a matter of "getting it right" (Poland, 2002)—that is, a matter of recording accurately every word that an interviewee and or interviewer utters. Transcription is, in fact, an interpretive act (Riessman, 2008).

Mishler (1991) uses the following example to make this point. In his paper, *Representing discourse: The rhetoric of transcription*, he compares and contrasts two verbatim transcriptions of 1.75 minutes of dialogue between a physician and his patient. In the first transcription, the dialogue is represented in sequences comprised of the physician's question, the patient's answer, followed by the physician's response. In the second transcription, the dialogue is represented in sequences comprised of the physician's question and the patient's answer. He notes that the first version of the transcription led to an examination of the adequacy of the patient's responses in relation to the physician's questions and to a conclusion emphasizing the physician's control over the discourse. The second version of the transcription led to a characterization of the views of the physician and the patient as equal and to a conclusion emphasizing the struggle in clinical conversations between "the voice of medicine" and "the voice of the lifeworld." Thus, the relationship between language and meaning is not transparent.

Two Notational Systems

The way in which oral speech is re-presented in text depends ultimately on the theoretical assumptions guiding the research as well as its aims. For example, conversation analysis, a method to study dialogue, requires transcriptions that include not only the words that are uttered but also *how* they are said (Silverman, 1993). Conversation analysis is concerned particularly with simultaneous and overlapping talk, pauses in talk, and characteristics of speech delivery such as prolongation and volume of sound because how something is said is considered central to understanding what it means (Atkinson & Heritage, 1984). The volume, *Structures of Social Action*, contains a clear description of how audio-recordings are transcribed for analysis by conversation analysts (Atkinson & Heritage, 1984); Jefferson (2004) also provides a useful account of this approach. The resulting texts that are produced are detailed and complex, and therefore the notational system is suitable for only brief stretches of talk.

By and large, the transcription conventions used in conversation analysis have not been used—or at least used in their entirety—in narrative research. However, at least one investigation has shown how re-transcription of a verbatim transcription of a narrative, whose meaning was ambiguous to include information pertaining to how the narrative was said, clarified its meaning (Clavarino, Najman, & Silverman, 1995). In an effort to preserve some of the advantages of the conversation-analytic notational system, following Poland (2002), Box 3–4 provides one approach to transcription that that would suit many narrative studies:

Box 3–4 Instructions for Transcribers

Record every word that is spoken. Do not summarize or paraphrase what you hear. Number every line of type. Use the words and symbols (i.e., the notational system) below every time you encounter a situation in which the relevant event occurs.

Event:	Notational System:
Pauses	Insert phrase, long pause, for pauses of four or more seconds (long pause), and insert phrase, short pause, for pauses of less than four seconds in parentheses (short pause); or insert specific length of pause in tenths of one second where (0.6) would indicate 6/10 of one second pause.
Expressive Sounds	Insert in parentheses the relevant word for a non-verbal communication such as (laughing), (crying), (sighing), for example
Interruptions	Insert a hyphen (-) in parentheses where interruption in speech occurs (He said that was impos-)
Overlapping speech	Insert a hyphen where interruption occurs and then insert in parentheses where overlapping speech occurs: R: He said that was impos-; (overlapping) I: Who said that? R: Bob
Garbled speech	Enclose in brackets a word that has been transcribed for one that was difficult to hear clearly [resigned] and use the letter, x, to indicate each word that cannot be understood at all (xxxx)

(Continued)

Box 3–4 Instructions for Transcribers (*Continued*)

Emphasis Use capital letters to denote emphasis through volume or pitch of speech, for example (WHAT?)

Held sounds Repeat sounds that are held, separated by hyphens (No-o-o-o)

Paraphrasing others Use quotation marks to indicate when the speaker is parodying what someone else said or expressing an inner voice (I thought "I'm in control now")

Source: Poland, B. (2002). Transcription quality. In J. Gubrium & J. Holstein (Eds), *Handbook of interview research: Context and method* (pp. 629–650). Thousand Oaks, CA: Sage.

Transcription Challenges

Whether or not the notational system displayed in Box 3–4 would be applicable to a given narrative study, however, depends on the level of linguistic and paralinguistic detail in which the investigator was interested. Whatever form of national system is employed, however, the accuracy with which the spoken words are transcribed is important. Specific challenges transcribers face when transcribing oral speech into written text include typing all the words that are spoken; including the correct word, rather than a similar word, that makes sense in relation to the entire text; and making defensible judgments regarding where to begin and where to end sentences or paragraphs (Poland, 2002).

Poland (2002) provides an example of the second challenge in this contrast between the words: "I have no doubt that communities are the way to go" (p. 631), in relation to an interview whose focus was health policy, and the words the transcriber heard and therefore typed: "I have no doubt that communities are the way to God!" He provides an example of the third challenge in this contrast between these sentences—"I hate it, you know. I do."—and the sentences—"I hate it. You know I do (p. 632)."

Enhancing Audio-Recording and Transcription Quality

In light of these complexities, strategies have been developed to enhance both the quality of audio-recordings and the accuracy with which they are transcribed. Patton (2002), for example, lists 21 suggestions for obtaining high-quality recordings, including the use of external microphones, testing the recording equipment with the respondent, and listening to the recording as soon as possible after the interview in order to provide the transcriber with names and terminology that might be unfamiliar.[2]

Poland (2002) discusses strategies for enhancing the accuracy of transcriptions recognizing all the while the problematic relationship between oral speech and written text and between representation and reality broadly defined. These strategies include providing clear instructions to transcribers with respect to the notational system to use, training transcribers to use the system, and reviewing the quality of their work. It takes a considerable amount of time to review each audio-recording against a transcription of the recording. As a result, one may choose to check only those recordings that a transcriber has identified as difficult to hear or to understand.

At the present time, transcribers charge about $30.00 for each hour of work. It takes a minimum of 4 hours for an experienced transcriber to produce a verbatim transcription of 1 hour of audio-recording. The length of time it takes to produce a verbatim transcription of 1 hour of audio-recording with paralinguistic communication included depends on the level of detail required. Investigators may prefer to listen to an audio-recording several times before deciding as to whether all of the recording should be transcribed.

Despite the importance of transcription as an interpretive research practice, some methods of narrative analysis are silent on this topic, others allude briefly to the importance of verbatim transcriptions, and others come with detailed instructions so that the transcription is treated explicitly as the first stage in the analysis of a story. However, irrespective of the analytic framework employed, I recommend that the investigator address transcription quality in research reports.

CONCLUSION

This chapter has elaborated a broad framework for the collection of data relevant to narrative studies by identifying the kinds of questions that might be posed in order to interpret fully the meaning of any narrative text.

It is unlikely that any one study would collect data with which to address of all of these questions, however. Thus, it is important for the investigator to consider what data, in addition to narrative data, he or she wishes to collect and why.

Nonetheless, standard practice in narrative research is for the interviewer to obtain high-quality audio-recordings of interviews; to record, upon completion of the interview, basic field notes regarding the conduct of the interview (that is, important characteristics of the interviewee, the interviewer, and the interview setting and process); and to produce a verbatim transcription of the interview that highlights unusual features of speech or nonverbal communication, such as shouting or pausing between words, that potentially alters the meaning of the words spoken. Field notes might also be taken in relation to how the interviewee and interviewer experienced the interview process, and these issues are explored further in Chapter 8 of this volume.

4

Analysis of Narrative Content

Developing an interpretation of narratives rather than a simple summary of narratives is a controversial undertaking. There are multiple approaches, and they have been classified in various ways (Langellier,
1989; Mishler, 1995; Riessman, 2008). In this chapter and in Chapters 5
and 7, I discuss major approaches to the analysis of narratives obtained
in the context of research interviews that hold potential for social work
research. They include ways to analyze the content of narratives, the
structure of narratives, and both in relation to the context in which they
occur.

The search for a defensible interpretive framework for a given
study is challenging. In the main, opportunities for the analysis of narratives collected for social scientific research have not been realized
(Atkinson & Delamont, 2006). This results in part from the uncritical
presumption that narratives of personal experience somehow "speak for
themselves" or represent "the truth of experience." Following Atkinson
and Delamont (2006), this volume is based on the presumption that the
adoption of an analytic stance toward narrative is required—indeed,
the narratives of the powerless, those with whom social work traditionally has engaged, as well as the powerful "equally deserve close analytic
attention (p. 170)."

INTRODUCTION

There are a variety of narrative data-analytic approaches through which investigators have examined the explicit or manifest content of narratives. Approaches include how to identify the pattern of one individual's life story (Liebich, Tuval-Mashiach, & Zilber, 1998); how to identify a pattern across multiple life stories (McAdams, 1999); how to examine the match between a widely known story within a subculture and the stories of its members (Cain, 1991); how to compare the fit between nonfictional and fictional narratives of the same experience (Landman, 2001; Shay, 1994); or how to evaluate the ways in which the events in a life shape and are shaped by the story told about that life (Rosenthal, 1998).

The overarching aim of these approaches is to capture a narrative's pattern, and as a result, they are ideal for study of topics of interest to social work, topics such as the evolution of post-traumatic stress disorder (Shay, 1994) or recovery from childhood sexual abuse, for example. They stand in contrast to perhaps the more familiar form of analysis of the content of texts of all sorts—content analysis (Krippendorf, 2004). Content analysis provides a way in which investigators may conceptualize all of the independent themes that are present in a narrative; it does not, however, provide a way for investigators to link those themes in relation to an evolving plot or story.

The three approaches, the approach of Lieblich and colleagues (Lieblich, Tuval-Mashiach, & Zilber, 1998), the approach of McAdams (1999), and the approach of Shay (1994), illustrated below show the power of these methods for study of social work-related problems.

HOLISTIC CONTENT ANALYSIS

Lieblich, Tuval-Mashiach, and Zilber (1998) refer to their approach to the interpretation of an entire life story, *holistic content analysis.*

Definition of Narrative

Lieblich and colleagues treat the life story generated within the context of one or more research interviews as narrative. Thus, they use the term, *narrative,* rather broadly, compared to other narrative analysts, to encompass the entire response of a research participant to an open-ended interview intended to elicit the participant's life story. They also use the term, *narrative*, to refer to their interpretation of the research participant's life story, reflecting the recognition that a social scientific report is a representation (or text) in its own right (Czarniawska, 2004).

Theoretical Orientation

The intent of their approach is to "*explore* and *understand* the *inner world* of individuals (p. 7)." They consider life story as neither a fiction nor an accurate representation of reality but rather a static product that is affected by the conditions under which it was produced and the cultural resources upon which the teller draws. The life story provided in a research interview, therefore, is a snapshot of an evolving story that changes throughout the life course.

They adopt a middle position with respect to the truth of life stories. Following Spence (1986), they consider a story as having a "narrative truth," which may vary with respect to the extent to which it conforms to "historical truth." Nonetheless, they assume that "stories are usually constructed around a core of facts or life events, yet allow a wide periphery for the freedom of individuality and creativity in selection, addition to, emphasis on, and interpretation of these 'remembered facts' (p. 8)."

The theoretical orientation of their narrative work is broadly psychological. They link the holistic content form of analysis specifically to the psycho-analytic work of Adler (1931), who emphasized the importance of *early memory* to understanding an individual's personality.

Central Question

The central question in the holistic content approach is: What is the core pattern in the life story?

Orientation to Method

To obtain a narrative suitable for holistic content analysis, the investigator conducts a life story interview. The authors' life story interview is similar to the one employed by McAdams (1985, 1993), whose work is described below. At the beginning of the interview, the interviewer introduces the task in the following manner:

> Every person's life can be written as a book. I would like you to think about your life now as if you were writing a book. First, think about the chapters of this book. I have here a page to help you in this task. Write down the years on the first column—from zero, from the day were born. When did the first stage [chapter] end? Write it here. Then go on to the next chapters, and put down the age that each one begins and ends for you. Go on till you reach your present age. You can use any number of chapters or stages that you find suitable to your own life (p. 25).

The interviewee is then asked to write a title for each chapter and to address the following questions for each one: "Tell me about a significant episode or a memory that you remember from this stage?" "What kind of a person were you during this stage?" "Who were significant people for you during this stage, and why?" and "What is your reason for choosing to terminate this stage when you did?"

It typically takes two interview sessions for interviewees to complete the interview; responses are tape-recorded and transcribed verbatim to include not only every word but also "affective expressions" such as sighing, crying, or laughing.

Lieblich and her colleagues note that it was helpful to their research team to meet regularly to sustain interest, improve skills, and enrich the ultimate analysis of the narrative data they obtained.

The transcribed data are then analyzed in the following five steps. *First*, the investigator reads the material repeatedly until he or she conceptualizes a pattern. The authors note that the global pattern usually presents itself as a focus for the entire story. *Second*, the investigator writes an initial impression of the life story. Initial impressions should include, for example, a general impression as to the core life story pattern as well as contradictions, unfinished descriptions, and issues that disturb the teller (p. 62). *Third*, the investigator identifies specific themes to follow within the story. Narrators often devote more time to important themes; however, omissions and brief references may also be critical to an interpretation of a life pattern (*see* Rogers et al., 1999, for a discussion of the language of the "unsayable").

The first three steps of the analysis depend on the explicit content of the life story. As a result, it is important to rely on the manifest content, what the narrator says, in order to complete these three phases of the analysis. The fourth and fifth steps in the analysis depend more heavily on the theoretical sensitivity the investigator brings to the analysis of the narrative. In the *fourth* step, the investigator reads the life story for each theme, marking each theme with a different colored marker, and then reads each one separately and repeatedly. For this step, Lieblich and colleagues adapted the procedure developed by Brown (Brown et al., 1988) for use in their work.[1] Identification and analysis of the narrator's earliest memories may be related to the thematic material and used to deepen the interpretation of the narrator's life story. In the *final* step, the investigator notes conclusions from the examination of each theme.

Major Concepts

The major concepts in this form of analysis are global impression, theme, early memory, and interpretive level. My reading of this approach is that the concept, *global impression*, is a broad one, intended to capture the overall pattern in an individual's life. In an analysis of one research participant's life story, for example, the authors frame the global impression in terms of life course "continuity," the centrality of relationships with others—especially women—the importance of family, and the narrator's positive evaluation of her life.

Themes are less global than the "global impression," and they are often stated in terms of opposites, such as belonging and separateness, which are repeated throughout the life story. The extent to which themes are cast in relation to theoretical concepts (i.e., their *interpretive level*) depends on the research purpose.

Themes may be understood in relation to a narrator's earliest memories. Lieblich and colleagues argue, following Adler (1931), that narrators create memories and construct them to reflect their current needs. As a result, *early memories* are an ideal tool with which to understand an individual and his or her foundational view of life. In general, however, Lieblich and colleagues attempt to be "naïve listener(s)" and not to impose theoretical constructs on the text.

ILLUSTRATION

Lieblich used this method to examine the narratives of young and middle-aged adults who had been enrolled in one of two types of post-primary school classroom experience (one in which immigrants were integrated with non-immigrant children and one in which the two groups were segregated) in Israel as part of a large-scale evaluation of the latter program. The developers of the program assumed the segregated program would have long-term effects on participants, and study investigators assumed these effects could be identified through narrative methods.

The authors use one story of a middle-aged man in their sample, the story of Jacob, to show how an early memory, the first story that he told the interviewer, in fact, may be used to illustrate the significance of a whole life. Jacob's memory, recorded in Box 4–1, is from late adolescence, and it pertains to an episode in which he tried, but failed, to save a fellow student who drowned (Lieblich, Tuval-Mashiach, Zilber, 1998, pp. 84–65).

In their evaluation of Jacob's story, Lieblich and colleagues note:

> It seems therefore the right place for beginning his life story, in spite of the fact that Jacob was already 17 at the time of its occurrence. One can describe his life as a circle, beginning in this episode at 17, continuing to mandatory [military] service a year later, returning to the army as a professional until the present time, and going back to his childhood memories, restructuring them to fit his choices . . . Looking closely at Jacob's early memory, two themes seem to be present in the narrative: providing aid to and rescuing others, and a courageous position during struggle (p. 86).

Box 4–1

And then I found myself . . . in a position of having to help my friends, take several people out of the water, one of them I pull out of the verge of–with us, or not with us. I, with another classmate, we turn him over and a huge quantity of water is coming out of him, and he returns to himself, and then I understand that actually I have faced for the first time a test of life and death, and I also helped whoever I could to save lives. . . .

Source: Lieblich, A., Tuval-Mashiach, R., Zilber, T. (1998). *Narrative research: Reading analysis, and interpretation.* London: Sage.

USE

Lieblich and colleagues refer to stories as being co-constructed by interviewers and interviewees, as drawing on cultural resources, or as infused with meaning that is not manifest in the explicit content of the stories told, but their approach does not allow a way in which to tackle these issues analytically. However, it does allow a contrast and comparison of narrated lives over time that holds potential to place, for example, social work interventions in context.

The work of Lieblich has evolved, and her students have published a paper that explores how narrators draw on societal knowledge to make sense of their lives: Schiff and Noy (2006), through a close reading of transcripts of interviews with a survivor of the Holocaust in World War II in Eastern Europe, show how a narrator uses a public figure, a war criminal she did not know, to communicate the nature of her persecutors and to convey how her experience differed from the experiences of survivors from Western Europe.

ANALYSIS OF NARRATIVE IDENTITY

The second approach to the analysis of narrative content I highlight is that of McAdams (1999). Along with Lieblich and colleagues, McAdams is interested in life pattern but he also focuses on the concept of identity. In the volume, *The Stories We Live By*, McAdams provides a lifespan developmental theory of how individuals create an identity through the stories that they tell (McAdams, 1993). Building, in part, on the work of Erikson (1968), the book defines identity in relation to a range of narrative concepts and then shows how each one arises at a particular point in the life cycle. In more recent work, McAdams casts identity construction as one of the five fundamental principles through which an integrative science of personality may be built (McAdams & Pals, 2006). I include his earlier work in this volume because this approach to identity is relevant to the advance of social work practice of many types.

Definition of Narrative

Although the term, *narrative*, is not defined explicitly in the 1993 work, McAdams defines the term, *story*, as a tale told in several episodes.

Each episode may be defined in relation to its setting, characters, an initiating event (an event to which a character responds with an effort to achieve a goal), and the consequence of the attempt, for example. The story builds over the course of several episodes to reveal a tension that must be resolved, or the *denouement*.

A personal myth is one kind of story that is created in adolescence and is revised throughout adulthood. It is a psychological structure that has conscious and unconscious elements. Unlike a story as defined above, a personal myth is an individual's identity and gives the individual a purpose and a place in the world. McAdams considers identity a preoccupation of individuals throughout most of adulthood. He cautions that although identity construction is an evolving process, individuals can never transcend the psychological, sociological, and cultural resources upon which identity construction relies.

Some identities, at least through middle adulthood, are considered more mature than others—personal myths that develop in the direction of coherence, openness, credibility, differentiation, reconciliation, and generative integration are considered to be more mature than those that do not.

Theoretical Orientation

McAdams' work on narrative identity is also informed by the work of philosopher, Paul Ricoeur (1991). Ricoeur emphasizes that human experience is storied and that we experience identity in story or narrative form. Ricoeur explains: "I am stressing the expression 'narrative identity' [because] . . . what we call subjectivity is neither an incoherent series of events nor an immutable substantiality, impervious to evolution. (p. 32)."

Thus, Ricoeur argues and McAdams (1993) agrees that we must understand identity with the same concepts that we might apply to the study of literature such as narrator, plot, and character, for example. Moreover, a narrative's meaning or, more specifically, an individual's narrative identity, does not reside in the text alone but rather in "*the intersection of the world of the text and the world of the reader* (italicized in the original) (Ricoeur, 1991, p. 26)." Thus, they must be brought together in order for understanding to occur (Squire, 2005).

Central Question

A central question in this approach to narrative is "What is the individual's identity?"

Major Concepts

The concepts McAdams uses to grasp an individual's identity include *narrative tone, personal imagery, thematic lines, ideological settings, pivotal scenes, and conflicting protagonists* (McAdams, 1993). Narrative tone refers to the narrator's faith in the possibilities of human behavior and motivation. Personal images represent a "synthesis of feeling, knowledge, and inner sensation, captured in an episode in time (p. 65)," and may be family images such as "the good mother" or religious images such as "the land of milk and honey." Theme refers to the narrator's primary aims. Aims are usually cast in relation to two supra-ordinate goals: love (communion) or power (agency). Ideological setting refers to the fundamental beliefs—especially religious and political—in which a story takes place.

The characters that dominate life stories are called *imagoes*. Imagoes are not people but rather are idealized ways that human beings may act; they might include, for example, idealizations as "the teacher", "the warrior", "the sage", "the caregiver", "the escapist", or "the survivor". Imagoes, however, may be idiosyncratic as well as common. They may be positive or negative, and they may reflect conflicting goals within an individual. In the latter case, they may be considered conflicting protagonists.

Orientation to Method

The intent in McAdams analysis of narratives is to understand "how the subject makes narrative sense of his or her life in the overall (McAdams, 2003, p. 214)." Thus, the emphasis is on semantics or what the narrative means.

To accomplish this aim, an interviewer asks a research participant a series of open-ended questions following the *Life Story Interview* protocol (McAdams, 1993). In this interview, the interviewer asks the research participant to describe the "chapters" of his or her life story, eight "key scenes in the story," a central life challenge, best and worst characters in the story, future chapters, basic values and beliefs exemplified by the story, and the central theme of the story considered as a whole.

The life story interview, an interview that takes about 2 hours to complete, is recorded and transcribed for analysis. I have not located specific transcription conventions in use in this method, however, the implication in the 1993 volume is that interviews are transcribed verbatim.

The interview text may be analyzed in one of two broad ways. First, the investigator may simply summarize the manifest content of the life story interview in order to understand, for example, how the individual describes the chapters of his or her life, a central life challenge, and best and worst characters in the story (see McAdams [1993] for one example of this sort of analysis). Or, the investigator may interpret the life story interview, considered as a whole, with the narrative concepts noted above in order to identify the research participant's identity.

Investigators may then compare and contrast individuals using one or more narrative concepts; they may conceptualize a common life story of a subgroup of particular interest; or they may link individual or common stories to prototypic stories within the culture of which the individual or group is a part.

ILLUSTRATION

An illustration of all the narrative concepts McAdams advances is beyond the scope of this volume. It is relevant to note, however, that scholars have used the concepts he has described to study issues of concern to social work practitioners: For example, the concept of conflicting protagonists has been applied to an analysis of the life story of a substance-dependent individual in a manner that expands understanding of habitual use of narcotics over the life course (Singer, 2001), and the concepts, chapters, plots, and imagoes, have been used to define a "reform narrative" of career criminals who desist from crime (Maruna, 1997).

USE

McAdams has used the narrative concepts discussed in his 1993 volume to pursue a broad range of questions as to the relationship between narrative and personality theory (McAdams, Hoffman, Mansfield, & Day, 1996), the relationship between narrative identity and personality traits and motives (McAdams, Anyidoho, Brown, Huang, Kaplan, & Machado, 2004), and the relationship between narrative themes and psychiatric conditions (Adler, Kissel, & McAdams, 2006). His current work at the Foley Center for the Study of Lives (www.sesp.northwestern.edu/foley) is dedicated to the study of adult development.

In his acclaimed volume, *The Redemptive Self,* McAdams (2006), drawing upon his narrative research with highly generative people in middle age and upon his analysis of stories of redemption drawn from contemporary American life and history, conceptualizes a quintessential American life story, a story of redemption, in which suffering is embraced, overcome, and transformed into something positive.

Despite the story's emphasis on optimism and a belief in the future, McAdams notes its potential limitations—the presumption of an innocent self, a sense of moral fervor or superiority, and a pursuit of celebrity, for example—that must be guarded against. Moreover, because some life events cannot be redeemed, he argues we need more complex stories "to do justice to the lived human experience and to suffering so intense and so pervasive that to hope for redemption in its wake is to trivialize the suffering itself (p. 262)." A tragic life story, he suggests, allows for such complexity to be revealed and for individuals to connect in deep empathy one to the other.

The Redemptive Self suggests how the articulation of a broad cultural story, such as the story of redemption, may be used to understand the life stories of individuals within the culture, such as stories told by those in recovery groups of all kinds. The volume also highlights the promises as well as the dangers such stories may hold.

McAdams conceptualization of narrative identity illustrates the advantages that Squire (2005) notes in relation to the hermeneutic strand of narrative analysis, of which the approach taken by McAdams (1993) is a part: It opens a way for scholars to join questions pertaining to biography to a method of narrative analysis.

On the other hand, the hermeneutic approach has limitations. Squire (2005), for example, questions the definition of story in relation to a linear conception of time and the certainty with which distinctions between "good" (mature) and "bad" (immature) narratives are drawn. She observes, for example:

> Perhaps it is an apparently unproblematic concept of time that underpins this certainty. The concept is complexly formulated in the Ricoeurian

tradition, but its fundamentality goes unquestioned. Personal narratives that sound spatialized, or that are purely theoretical . . . or that seem "outside" biographical time . . .[for example] in my South African interviews . . . [a woman's] . . . account of her life in terms of ancestor myths and dreams . . . get interpretively translated into lived temporality. These translations impose time itself as an interpretive category and, more narrowly, standards of progression and ending, and may close off spaces of both the unconscious and the real. A kind of displaced realism gets played out in this valuing of well-arranged, well-"timed" stories for their own sake . . . (p. 99).

Shay, the scholar to whose work I now turn, examines episodic narratives told over a long period of time but interpreted in relation to a tragic story of the sort McAdams may have had in mind when he advanced their potential for understanding suffering.

CONSTRUCTION OF A SHARED NARRATIVE[2]

Shay, a psychiatrist who has worked with veterans of the Vietnam War, wrote the volume *Achilles in Vietnam: Combat Trauma and the Undoing of Character* (Shay, 1994). In this volume, his intent was neither to introduce nor to illustrate a new method of narrative analysis but rather to illuminate for the public the catastrophic nature of the experience of war.

Working with the stories that he heard from veterans in the therapeutic groups he conducted as part of an outpatient program in which he worked over an extended period of time, he began to identify a common story or, as he says, a "composite voice." He enlarged the meaning of the common story through a comparison and contrast of that story with the one told by Homer in the Greek epic, the *Iliad* (Homer, nd/1974), an epic that is over 27 centuries old. To illustrate the points that he makes throughout the work, however, he relies on "single voices" or stories individual veterans told, described in writing, or that were reconstructed by the author from his notes.

The work displays the experience of war and its aftermath. It shows how the experiences of soldiers, separated by vast differences in time and culture, were the same but also differed and that the differences resulted from the structure and organization of the U.S. Army in Vietnam.

I include Shay's work in this volume because it shows how one clinician engaged in narrative inquiry. (In addition, it is worth noting that this work promoted a fundamental reassessment within the U.S. Army as to the use of rotation and the centralization of command (www.nytimes.com/2003/03/11/science/scient-work-jonathan-shay), thereby suggesting that social scientific concerns with validity or trustworthiness, however these terms are defined, may recede in the presence of work that creates not only a space in which a compelling story may be told but also an audience willing to listen [Plummer, 1995].)

Definition of Narrative

Shay does not define narrative. Instead, he relies on a common-sense understanding of a narrative as a story, and he provides multiple examples of veterans' accounts of their war experiences within *Achilles in Vietnam*.

Theoretical Orientation

Shay reflects a social constructivist approach to narrative, an approach that assumes that the narrator's identity may vary in relation to his or her context and that the narrator and the narrative are inseparable from the social context of which they are a part. However, his clinical approach is informed by a psychodynamic understanding of trauma and narrative and the difficulty many survivors have "in putting their experience into words (p. 191)."

The theoretical orientation of his approach to the analysis of narratives is not stated; however, he attends carefully to classicists' understandings of the *Iliad* and veterans' understandings of their experience in combat. He writes, for example:

> I respect the work of classical scholars and could not have done my work without them. Homer's poem does not mean whatever I want it to mean. However, having honored the boundaries of meaning that scholars have pointed out, I can confidently tell you that my reading of the *Iliad* is not a "meditation" that is only tenuously rooted in the text (p. xx).

Central Question

The central question that animates this work is this: What is the meaning of long-term combat in Vietnam for middle-aged veterans of that conflict?

Major Concepts

The major concepts and assumptions underlying this approach to analysis of narratives are intertwined with Shay's approach to treatment of post-traumatic stress disorder. For example, he states that *listening* to the stories must precede any kind of analysis. Moreover, the type of listening he has in mind requires persistent engagement with narrators and a refusal to classify too soon their experience. He writes:

> All too often . . . our mode of listening deteriorates into intellectual sorting, with the professional grabbing the veterans' words from the air and sticking them into mental bins . . . Passages of narrative here contain the particularity of individual men's experiences, bearing a different order of meaningfulness than any categories they might be put into (pp. 4–5).

Part of the meaningfulness to which he alludes is the meaningful of stories told by individuals who have suffered great harm and the compelling nature of the tales they have to tell. Through sustained and repeated listening to veterans' narratives and contrast and comparison of these narratives with the story of Achilles, Shay conceptualized the common *themes* that reflected how ancient and contemporary soldiers experienced long-term heavy combat.

The narratives also display, despite their individuality, the shared military *culture* in which the soldiers operated. Shay uses the traces of this culture within both the *Iliad* and veterans' stories to describe and to interpret its significance for the individual soldier. Military culture, "ancient or modern," is treated as a social construction in which stories must be understood.

Orientation to Method

Shay obtained veterans' narratives, either spoken, written, or constructed from his field notes; conceptualized the common experience of war;

enlarged his understanding of the common experience through a comparison and contrast of veterans' common experience with that of Achilles, highlighting both what was the same and what was different; and then considered the implications of his analysis for clinical and military practice.

The book is structured around the experience of war *over time* and chapter headings reflect the process through which soldiers came to feel betrayed and to enter the berserk state. Thematic categories include, for example, "betrayal of 'what's right'"; "shrinkage of the social and moral horizon"; "grief at the death of a special comrade"; "guilt and wrongful substitution"; "berserk"; and "dishonoring the enemy." Each is illustrated with extensive quotes from individual veterans.

In describing the berserk state, for example, he quotes the words of one veteran recorded in Box 4–2, speaking of the death of a "friend in arms" (Shay, 1994, p. 96).

Shay elaborates the way in which berserking "American soldiers invariably shed their helmets and flak jackets. They had no other armor . . . All the berserker feels he needs is a weapon (p. 97)." Shay then turns to a passage in the *Illiad* in which Achilles wishes to kill Hektor, after hearing the death of his "friend in arms," Patroklos. Shay observes:

> Once we grasp the psychological attractiveness of going into battle naked, the following passage makes complete sense, when Achilles roars at his mother: "Do not attempt to keep me from the fight, though you love me; you cannot make me listen." (18:146f) He remembers well that he has no armor; only a moment before he told his mother this, but he still has his great Pelian spear (p. 97).

Box 4–2

And we looked and looked and looked. And the only thing that was left was, it almost looked like a wig. It was just his hair. Just his hair. And we put that in the body bag. And I was crying like a baby. . . And I cried and I cried and I cried. . . . And I stopped crying. And I probably didn't cry again for twenty years. I turned. I had no feelings. I wanted to hurt. I wanted to hurt. And I wanted to hurt.

Source: Shay, J. (1994). *Achilles in Vietnam: Combat trauma and the undoing of character.* New York: Scribner.

In the third part of the volume, Shay shows how the devastation of war promotes not only post-traumatic stress disorder but also the undoing of character. He argues that soldiers and veterans need to tell stories about war in order to communalize the experience and to achieve personal healing.

His work conflates a well-known distinction drawn by Polkinghorne (1995) between the collection of descriptions of *events* and other happenings to create a narrative that explains them and the collection of *stories* to reduce them to categories or typologies. It also illustrates the power of narrative inquiry to open up interdisciplinary study of a phenomenon, and Shay's work on this issue has appeared in the journals *Nature, The American Journal of Physiology, Ancient Theatre Today, and Parameters: Journal of the U.S. Army War College* (www.nytimes.com/2003/03/11/sciences/scientist-at).

ILLUSTRATION

Another study that relies on a literary work to illuminate personal change is the study by Landman (2001). Unlike Shay, Landman uses explicit narrative concepts to examine the process through which individuals undergo ethical transformation. Relying on the concepts *protagonist-in-context/protagonist-in-ideological setting, the predicament, the struggle with the predicament/consequences, outcome/denouement* (McAdams, 1993; Robinson & Hawpe, 1986), *and epilogue,* Landman compared and contrasted the central figure in Dostoevsky's novel, *Crime and Punishment* (Dostoevsky, 1866/1989), and the real-life character of Katherine Ann Power, who lived underground for two decades and was prosecuted, imprisoned, and paroled for her actions in relation to her resistance to the Vietnam War.

Dostoevsky's novel and transcribed interviews with (or stories written about) Powers were the narratives with which Landman worked. Through a close reading of these narratives and other historical materials, Landman described the historical, cultural, and ideological context in which both characters were operating, the core convictions behind their crimes, the emotional consequences of the crimes, and the outcomes for each protagonist. In so doing, she conceptualized how regret, guilt, and shame may be transformed, after having done serious harm to others.

She observed, for example, that Powers and the character created by Dostoevsky "share the crucial conviction that the greater good sometimes requires the independent thinker to engage in acts that lie outside the law and conventional morality (Landman, 2001, p. 45)." Thus, the *predicament* each faced was between a desire to promote the well-being of a community and the belief that the only means to do so was to break the laws of the community. However, profound shame, alienation from others, acts of self-punishment, frantic activity to ward off suicide, efforts at atonement and urges to confess, and eventual confession and imprisonment followed violating the law for both.

Landman highlights three insights such a comparative analysis revealed *One*, the basis for transformation is emotional rather than primarily rational. Thus, dealing directly with regret, guilt, and shame are central to rehabilitation. *Two*, circumstances play a powerful role in life and such circumstances, although they do not absolve individuals from responsibility for their actions, are critical to understanding them. *Three*, "what happens out in the human community-confession, atonement, expiation through acceptance of *society's* penance in a 'penitentiary' and eventual reunion with humanity (p. 64)" is as important as what happens within individuals. The work highlights how suffering may be redemptive and suggests the attention that might be given to the moral dimensions of social work practice.

USE

The approach is best suited for studies of profound relational experiences, and it should rely on literary works that have stood the test of time. Although I have not been able to identify many such investigations, a plethora of literary works stand ready for exploration in relation to topics of keen interest to social work scholars, works such as Henry Roth's examination of a child's experience of immigration and cultural conflict in the volume, *Call it Sleep* (Roth, 1934/1991), or Thomas Hardy's portrait of a mother's experience of child loss in the context of grinding poverty and a patriarchal and class-bound society in the volume, *Tess of the d'Urbervilles* (Hardy, 1891/2008), for example.

This approach is powerful because the authors of the literary works chosen for analysis are gifted and the contemporary narrators are insightful and forthcoming. As a result, a direct comparison of the explicit content of the mythic or fictional and nonfictional stories is possible and contains the power to inform both theory and practice.

In other situations, however, contemporary narrators hesitate, hedge, or remain silent when telling stories of their lives (Chamberlayne & King, 2000; Rosenthal, 1993, 1998; Wengraf, 2001). Although complex and not amenable to summary in a volume that surveys narrative methods, the biographic-interpretive method, a method developed by Gabriele Rosenthal and Wolfram Fischer-Rosenthal in Germany over the past several decades, specifically addresses this issue. The core papers are written in German; however, Rosenthal has published at least one methodological paper (Rosenthal, 1993) and one book (Rosenthal, 1998) in English, the influential volume, *The Holocaust in Three Generations*. This approach reflects the strong presence of biographical work in that country and, because of the Nazi era, concerns regarding evasion or lies in relation to difficult times (Merrill & West, 2009). Investigators working with this method have continued to pursue investigations in Europe and in the United States (www.uni-goettingen.de/en).

CONCLUSION

This chapter has highlighted three approaches to the analysis of the content of narratives, holistic content analysis, analysis of narrative identity, and construction of a common narrative. Taken together, they provide a wide range of concepts that are useful for the study of individual narratives, the comparison of narratives across cases, and for the construction of a common narrative from interviews with a relatively large number of research participants who have experienced the same phenomenon.

With the exception of the biographic-interpretive method noted above, these approaches tend to assume that the meaning of what people say is relatively transparent, that there is a unitary and an agentic subject behind the story that is told, and that the stories they tell are coherent rather than fragmented, ambiguous, or contradictory (*see* the work of Sclater, 1998, for one example of a study of contradiction in narrative). This approach runs the risk of cutting "researchers off from all the other literary and cultural studies work on narrative which takes more complicated approaches to subjectivity (Squire, 2008, p. 54)."

Moreover, they tend to ignore the significance of how individuals tell their stories for what they mean. Structural approaches to the analysis of narratives, by way of contrast, are grounded in the assumption that understanding how a narrative is structured is central to understanding its meaning, and it is to these approaches that I turn in the chapter to follow.

5

Analysis of Narrative Structure

Analytic methods that focus on the structure of a narrative focus on its form rather than primarily its content. The underlying assumption of this family of approaches is that understanding the structure of a narrative is central to understanding its meaning.

One important distinction in this set of data-analytic techniques is between narrative-analytic approaches that focus on the *underlying structure* of a text and those that focus on its *surface* (Gulich & Quasthoff, 1985). In the former category, one would include the work of Propp (1928/1968), who studied structure in relation to the acts of characters and their significance for the story as a whole; Greimas (Greimas & Courtés, 1982), who studied structure in relation to changes of state in a narrative; and Mandler (1984), who studied plots in use in specific interpretive communities (as cited in Czarniawska, 2004). In the latter category, analytic approaches that focus on the surface of a text, one would include the work of Labov and Waletsky (1967), who studied the order in which clauses appeared in a narrative, and Gee (1991), who studied a narrative's poetic structure.

INTRODUCTION

Structural methods of analysis have been used to study topics of interest to social work, including, for example, caregiving (Poindexter, 2002,

2003), although their potential has yet to be realized within the profession. To illustrate these methods, this section focuses on the work of three scholars—Labov (Labov & Waletsky, 1967; Labov, 1972), Gee (1991), and Gregg (2006). Labov and Gee focus on the surface structure of narrative, whereas Gregg focuses on both the surface and the deep structure.

ANALYSIS OF SEQUENCE IN NARRATIVE

The work of Labov has been described as the narrative canon (Georgakopoulou, 2006; Nicolopoulou, 1997)—a theory and approach to narrative that has dominated the field and against which many social scientists engaged with narrative compare and contrast their work. Although the model has changed somewhat over time (Labov & Waletsky, 1967; Labov, 1972; Labov, 1982; Labov, 1997), the original formulation provided a starting point for a wide range of studies that utilize narrative (as cited by Patterson, 2008).

Definition of Narrative

Within this framework, a narrative is defined as one in which a narrator recounts a personal experience of a *specific event* that occurred in the past in the order in which the event occurred in real life. The interest is in events that are "an important part of the speaker's biography" (Labov, 1997), that are reportable (i.e., that require an explication), and that are of interest to others.

Labov's definition of narrative assumes that a narrative is temporally ordered with a beginning, middle, and end; that it refers to events that are true; and that it is told to an audience who has not heard the story before but who will understand its meaning (Georgakopoulou, 2006).[1] It is further assumed that this understanding will depend ultimately on a shared socio-linguistic context and not on details contained in the story.

Theoretical Orientation

The original intent behind this work was to understand relatively brief and simple narratives as a beginning step toward understanding social class differences in the structure and function of more complex narratives (Labov & Waletsky, 1967); thus, it was grounded in sociolinguistics.

Central Question

The central question with which Labov is concerned has evolved over the course of his qualitative work on narrative. The early work (Labov & Waletsky, 1967), the primary focus in this volume, addressed the question: What is a narrative? Or, as Mishler (1986a) reframed the question, "How can we isolate the essential 'narrative structure' from the flow of talk? (p. 79)."

Major Concepts

In the Labovian approach, a *fully formed narrative* is comprised of the following six elements: Abstract (A), Orientation (O), Complicating Action (CA), Evaluation (E), Resolution or Result (R), and Coda (C) (Labov, 1972, p. 363). The Abstract is a summary of the story to come; the Orientation provides the setting (who, when, where); the Complicating Action indicates what happened next; the Evaluation indicates the point of the story; the Result states what finally happened; and the Coda indicates the story is over and the narration returns to the present time. These elements are present because oral narratives of personal events must contain the information that establishes the credibility of a narrative to the audience to whom it is being told.

Box 5–1 presents an example of one such narrative drawn from my study of abusive and or neglectful mothers who lost custody of their children (Wells, 2007). In this example, the words of the narrator that were said loudly or were shouted are capitalized.

Not all narratives contain all six elements. *Core narratives* are comprised of just one element, the Complicating Action, and *a minimal narrative* is comprised of two independent clauses that are temporally ordered such that a reversal of the two would change the meaning of the story. Following this definition, for example, the two clauses: "I punched this boy/and he punched me back" constitute a narrative because the reversal of the two: "This boy punched me/and I punched him back" (Labov, 1972, p. 360) alters its meaning.

Although the evaluation clause was considered originally as a discrete element, Labov (1972) later noted that evaluation may be spread throughout the story and that it may involve—either implicitly or explicitly—a comparison of what happened with what might have happened (Labov, 1997; Patterson, 2008). Evaluation clauses may be of three types: *external* (i.e., the narrator stops the action and steps outside the action in order to evaluate it), *embedded* (i.e., the narrator continues the action but records a feeling), or *evaluative* (i.e., the narrator reports action that reveals emotion without the use of speech) (Patterson, 2008). For example, the evaluation in Box 5–1 is an external evaluation.

Box 5–1

ABSTRACT (A):

1. I didn't have anyone, and
2. I really didn't have a home.

ORIENTATION (O):

3. I was passing on the Fourth of July, I was walking past someone.
4. They were in their backyard with their, with their children running.

COMPLICATING ACTION (CA):

5. And I felt this big, I felt like I could have just walked off into the sea or . . .
6. you know, I just felt disgusted, real yucky with myself . . . and hurt
7. and I passed that house

EVALUATION (E):

8. and I looked
9. and I said, "One day that's how my family going to be." One day.

RESOLUTION (R):

10. I never will forget that.
11. That was one of the most . . . And it . . . that, you know,
12. I never thought that. I mean, walking up the street that I would meet myself like that,
13. or meet that feeling . . . like that.

CODA (C):

14. And that is one crazy . . . feeling I never want to go back to. NEVER.

Source: Wells, K. (December, 2007). The experience of custody loss: Preliminary narrative analysis of one mother's report. Invited presentation, Chapin Hall Center for Children, University of Chicago, Chicago, IL.

Orientation to Method

To obtain narrative data, an interviewer asks a question such as the one Labov (1972) asked in his study of the Black vernacular style: "Were you ever in a situation where you were in serious danger of being killed, where you said to yourself—'This is it?' (p. 354)." If the respondent responds affirmatively to such a question, the interviewer then poses an open-ended question such as: What happened?

The responses are audio-recorded and transcribed to produce a verbatim text, a text that may also contain other kinds of speech, including descriptions, reports, or argumentation. Material that is clearly irrelevant to the narrative is eliminated.

Then, each independent clause in the remaining text is identified and tested to determine whether its movement to a different position in the account would alter its meaning. If a clause cannot be moved, it is considered a narrative clause, and it must remain in the order in which it occurs in the account, and it comprises the Complicating Action.

The narrative and the remaining clauses in the account are then numbered and categorized into one of the six elements in the model. To do so, Labov recommends the "question method." "This [method] is based on the idea that a narrative can be understood as a series of answers to the underlying questions that all narratives address. The clauses within a narrative thus function to answer different questions (Patterson, 2008, p. 25)." These questions are: What is the story about? (the Abstract [A]); Who is involved, when, and where? (the Orientation [O]); And then what happened? (the Complicating Action [CA]); What is the point? (the Evaluation [E]); and What finally happened? (the Resolution [R]) Rather than answer a question, the Coda (C) returns the story to the present time.

To clarify the narrator's perspective on the "bare bones" of what actually happened, the evaluation clauses are removed and then re-introduced into the narrative. Mishler (1986a) provides one useful example of how this parsing is done.

Box 5–2 presents an example of a minimal narrative provided by Patterson (2008, p. 35). The text is from a woman describing her life to her therapist after a physical assault. In this text, underlining refers to a word emphasized by the narrator; a dot enclosed in parentheses (.) refers to a discernible pause in talk typically considered less than two-tenths of a second.

The material in Box 5–2 contains an example of the way in which the Labovian model treats narrative as text. Words are emphasized, but the way in which the words are said (or performed) and the context in which they are uttered is not (Mishler, 1986a). This is because Labov considers oral narratives of specific events involving moral injury or death to be monologues over which the narrator has limited control (Labov, 1972). Indeed, he argues that the narrator is compelled to replay automatically such events because the narrator is rehearsing or reliving events in the past in a way that the occasion for the production of the narrative becomes relatively unimportant (Squire, 2005).

USE OF LABOVIAN NARRATIVES

Once a narrative is identified, a key question is: What does the narrative mean? The evaluation component of the Labovian model contains the narrator's explicit assessment of the story's meaning and, as such, is one answer to the question (Langellier, 1989). The evaluation contains the soul of the narrative.

Labov's work suggests other directions the analyst may pursue to address this question, including an examination of the way in which

Box 5–2	
1. there was an incident actually a few weeks ago	A/O
2. I was with my mother-in-law and my daughter and the little girl from next door (.)	O
3. we were walking the dog	O
4. and there was a man	O
5. who was sitting (.) erm (.)	O
6. drinking a bottle of wine or sherry or something	O
7. looking very er (.) well down (.) dirty and shabby	O
8. but he had that <u>look</u> (.)	O
9. and he <u>watched</u> (.)	CA
10. as we passed very intensely (.)	CA
11. <u>now</u> if I hadn't been with my mother-in-law	E
12. I would have been absolutely (.) scared out of my mind	E
13. but because she was there you know	E
14. I felt OK (.) just about (.)	R
15. she was worried . . .	R

Source: Patterson, W. (2008). Narratives of events: Labovian narrative analysis and its limitations. In M. Andrews, C. Squire, & M. Tamboukou (Eds.), *Doing narrative research* (pp. 22–40). London: Sage.

praise and blame are represented in the story; a contrast and comparison of narratives across cases; or a consideration of how narratives are related to actual behavior (Labov, 1982). (For example, Labov showed how narratives of violent events, when reduced to their essential structure, were comprised of a request and a response to the request that stigmatized the individual making the request and provoked him to violence (Mishler, 1986a). This analytic approach moves Labov's work away from an emphasis on the surface structure of a story to the deep structure or the function of events in the overall narrative.) Or, one may appeal to other parts of the interview to clarify the full meaning of the story told, as was the case for Patterson (2008) in her analysis of the woman's story reported above.

In his most recent work (Labov, 2010), Labov has examined how a storyteller knows where a story should begin, emphasizing that every story requires a decision as to where in the chain of causal events to begin the tale.

ILLUSTRATION

Riessman (1990) illustrated and supplemented Labovian analysis in her volume, *Divorce Talk: Women and Men Make Sense of Personal Relationships*. In this study, she examined respondents' narratives of their reasons for divorce. (She identified not only the narratives that met Labov's criteria but also what she called habitual narratives [narratives that refer to a chronic state]; hypothetical narratives [narratives that refer to possible events or circumstances]; and episodically structured narratives [narratives comprised of several episodes which vary in thematic content].)

Her analysis shows how narrative structure and meaning may be linked. For example, one respondent, Tessa, in response to Riessman's directive to state the "main causes of your separation, as you see it," replied with a long account in which several types of narratives were embedded, including narratives that met Labov's criteria for narrative.

Comparing and contrasting the narratives of multiple respondents, Riessman illustrated how the same reason for divorce carried different implications for those involved. She explained:

> A case in point was a spouse's infidelity, a "reason" given by a group of participants. Using Labov's model, I compared how three participants combined story elements in contrasting ways because they had such

different points to make about the relationship of their spouse's (long-term) affairs to their divorces. What, on the surface, appeared to be the same events turned out to be quite different ones . . . (Riessman, 2008, p. 87).

In this way, Riessman contributed not only to our understanding of marriage and divorce but also to our understanding of the limitations of content analysis for the development of knowledge.

USE

Labov argues that through close study of vernacular and casual speech, we may enlarge our understanding of individuals' perspectives and of social life. Such close study also has implications for professional practice. For example, Labov's (1972) volume, *Language in the Inner City: Studies in the Black English Vernacular*, was designed explicitly to challenge the theory that the language of Black children was an obstacle to learning and to logical thinking (Riessman, 2008). By showing how children's language was both coherent and sophisticated, this work provided knowledge that professionals could use to understand children's views.

The Labovian framework has several advantages: It allows identification of narratives within interviews; comparison of narratives across interviews, especially with respect to evaluation clauses; elucidation of the narrator's perspective (Patterson, 2008); and consideration of how narrative functions in varying ethnic and social class contexts.

However, the assumptions underlying the framework do not always hold. For example, Sands (2004) found that when she tried to use the framework to identify stories told within the context of one long interview, that they "were not discrete entities that fit neatly into Labov's model, but rather were spread out, repeated, and linked to other stories, and formed episodes of a larger story (p. 54)."

This difficulty may result from unacknowledged effects of the interviewer and interview context on the narration (Mishler, 1986a) or from the presence of ambiguous or contradictory stories. Indeed, Georgakopoulou (2006) has argued the Labovian model should be replaced with one that acknowledges the dynamic nature of narrative and that narrative inquiry should focus on how narrative emerges in dialogue, over time, and in relation to communicative contexts so that fragmented or contingent narratives may be understood.

Scholars have suggested modifications to Labov's approach (Polanyi, 1985) or have clarified conditions under which other approaches might be more useful (Patterson, 2008; Riessman, 1993). Riessman (1993) used the approach of Gee (1991), a method to which I now turn, to analyze narratives in which events may play a role but that center on emotional reactions and subjective experience.

ANALYSIS OF POETIC STRUCTURE OF NARRATIVES

Gee (1985) is interested in "oral strategy narratives" rather than "topic-centered narratives" that unfold in a temporally ordered sequence (Riessman, 2008).

Definition of Narrative

The oral narratives of interest are those in which the story is told in a series of loosely linked segments; the segments may shift with respect to characters, location, and time; and the relationships among the segments must be inferred by the listener because the narratives may give the initial impression of lacking a point. Stories told by individuals in some socio-cultural groups (Gee, 1991) or some individuals under duress might fall in this category.

Theoretical Orientation

Working within the tradition of socio-linguistics, Gee (1991) argues that much may be learned regarding the meaning of such narratives from a study of how they are said or their *poetic structure*. Thus, the focus is on how a narrative is spoken in units that occur naturally in speech (Riessman, 2008).

Riessman (2008) cautions that Gee's approach "is founded on a North American English prosodic system of stress and pitch, dictating how he . . . [analyses] a text. Applications to speech samples from other languages and other English prosodic systems must be attempted cautiously (p. 94)."

Central Question

By attending to how a story is told, or its structure, the investigator may infer a defensible interpretation of its meaning. Thus, the central question in this approach is: What is a defensible interpretation of the meaning of an oral narrative?

Gee (1991) notes, however, that there may be more than one such interpretation: "[t]here will, of course, usually be several acceptable answers, differing by the sorts of contextual knowledge the interpreter brings to the job of interpretation. But many answers are ruled out by the structure of the . . . [story] (p.16)."

Orientation to Method

Gee's narrative analytic procedure involves the following steps:

First, listen carefully and repeatedly to an audio-recording of the story; examine the story in relation to a verbatim transcription of the story; and, then, relying on both, identify the text that is *focused*, that is, the material that is said with a prominent pitch (i.e., the voice rises, falls, rises and falls, or falls and rises in relation to the normal pitch of the sentence) that signals the information the speaker wants to emphasize. A sentence with one pitch glide (or change in pitch) is called an *idea unit*.

Second, mark the text into numbered *lines* comprised of one or two idea units, separated by a slash, that contain one central idea.

Third, mark the lines into *stanzas*—stanzas focus on a single topic, pertain to one scene, present a take on a character or claim, or constitute a change from a preceding stanza.

Fourth, identify the stanzas that are *strophes*, or stanzas that are in related pairs.

Fifth, identify the larger *parts* of the story into which the strophes fall. Stanzas, strophes, and parts are labeled to reflect content of the story.

Box 5–3 presents the first 12 of 64 lines of Gee's (1991) analysis of a verbatim transcription of an uninterrupted story told by a young woman with schizophrenia. This text demonstrates the first five steps in his analysis. Taken directly from Gee (1991, pp. 17–18), each line is comprised of

---

Box 5–3

Part 1 (The sea)
Strophe 1 (Storms)
Stanza 1 (Play in thunderstorms)

1. Well when I was LITTLE / the MOST EXCITING thing that we used to do is
2. There used to be THUNDERSTORMS on the beach that we lived on
3. And we walked down to MEET the thunderstorms
4. And we'd turn around and RUN HOME / running AWAY from the / running away from the THUNDERSTORMS

Stanza 2 (Play in waves from storms)

5. That was the MOST EXCITING / one of the MOST EXCITING times we ever had was doing things like that
6. Besides having like when there was HURRICANES OR STORMS out on the ocean
7. The WAVES / they would get really BIG
8. And we'd go down and PLAY in the waves when they got big

Strophe 2 (Waves)
Stanza 3 (Waves big: Up and down)

9. And one summer the waves were ENORMOUS
10. They were just about / they went STRAIGHT UP AND DOWN
11. So the SURFERS WOULDN'T ENJOY them or anything like that
12. They'd just go STRAIGHT up and down / the HUGEST HUGEST things in the world

Source: Gee, J. (1991). A linguistic approach to narrative. *Journal of Narrative and Life History*, 1(1), 15–39. Reprinted with permission from Elsevier.

---

one or more idea units, separated from each other by a slash. Material that "is 'focused' (said with a prominent pitch) is capitalized, and the 'main line' parts of the plot are underlined (p. 17)."

Major Concepts

Drawing on the analytic steps and related concepts defined above, Gee poses five *levels of textual structure*, each of which promotes an interpretation of the meaning of the text. *Level 1*, the line and stanza structure, is comprised of the lines and stanzas as defined above. *Level 2* is the syntax and cohesion structure. Syntax refers to the way in which words integrate material within and across lines and that may be used to switch topics or to enhance contrasts. Cohesion refers to the ways in which lines and stanzas are linked. Thus, a primary question with which the investigator is concerned at this level is: What connections does the narrator make? *Level 3* is comprised of two parts, the plot (i.e., the main events of the plot contained in the main clauses of the narrative) and the off-line plot (i.e., "the states, generic events, repeated events, and habitual events [p. 14]").

The investigator uses *Levels 1, 2,* and *3* in relation to *Level 4,* the psychological subjects, and *Level 5,* the focusing system, to develop a full interpretation of the meaning of the text. The psychological subject, the grammatical subject of the main clauses, represents the "points of view from which the material in a stanza is viewed; they represent what the narrator is 'empathizing' with (Kuno & Kaburaki, 1977) (Gee, 1991, p. 30)." The focusing system is comprised of the central topics or themes contained in and across the lines of the text. The primary question with which the analyst is concerned at this level is: Why are the themes important?

A successful analysis is one that allows the analyst to reconstruct part of the narrator's philosophy of life. For example, Part 1 of the young woman's story reported above continues with a description of the power of the waves. Part 2 includes a description of the next exciting thing (riding horses); working in order to ride horses for free; being afraid of riding; overcoming fear of riding; growing mastery of riding. Part 3 includes a description of taking the horses into the sea; riding the horses to a country store and to camp; other girls at camp being rich and afraid of horses and of the narrator; becoming afraid of horses and leaving camp; and having a good time when young.

Gee summarizes the progression of themes or images in the entire narrative as "*We* play with powerful sea/*I* work to master powerful horses/*We* play in sea with horses (equate sea + horses + power + being member of the group)/*Rich girls* afraid of horses/power/narrator (equate horses + power + narrator)/*I* afraid of girls/horses/power/self/*I* separate from group/*I* unafraid then (p. 36)."

Using this analytic system, Gee works toward an interpretation that renders the narrative "deeply senseful"—a story in which the narrator's mastery is undone by fear of others and isolation—"her world of innocence—running to meet thunderstorms, riding bareback in the sea—is gone (p. 36)."

The power of Gee's approach may not be immediately obvious until the investigator reads a verbatim transcription of a story. Riessman (2008) recounts that after reviewing a transcription of the story Gee analyzes, her students find "the speech sample 'strange,' even incoherent; one social work student said the woman had 'a thought disorder.' Given that the tape of the woman's speech was given to Gee 'as an example of a text that made little overall coherent sense to those who had collected it,' my students' responses were not unique . . . (p. 94)."

It is important to note that Gee's point, at the time he was writing the manuscript to which this section refers, was not that the context in which the narrative is embedded is unimportant. It is that the significance of the structure of a narrative to its meaning had been unappreciated.

ILLUSTRATION

Edvardsson, Rasmussen, and Riessman (2003) provide an example of this approach. They report a study of one woman's story of her positive and negative experiences in hospitals, focusing specifically on the atmosphere of hospital wards. Using an adaptation of Gee's approach to an analysis of how the narrator told her story, the authors develop an interpretation as to its meaning; conceptualized four broad domains of social contexts of hospital wards that facilitated healing; specified these contexts in terms of specific actions of the hospital staff; and then linked their conceptualization to the extensive literature on the topic.

Edvardsson and his colleagues also note how their detailed examination of the narrator's retelling of her experiences of "horror and healing" helped them (and by extension, the readers of the article) to understand her moral point, a critical function of research within the professions.

Indeed, Crepeau's (2000) study of narratives, co-constructed over time by treatment providers for one psychiatric patient, shows how professionals in the helping professions may be unaware of the power of the moral points of the stories they tell. The author observes:

> From these stories, different moral tales emerge so that the right actions for a particular patient may be taken. Unfortunately, team members typically do not recognize this imagistic or constructive process. This lack of awareness means that they are not likely to recognize the

thematic and moral components of their discussion and how these contribute to their clinical reasoning and subsequent decision making (p. 784).

USE

The approach of Gee has been widely influential, and it has been adopted (Riessman, 2008) or adapted by many scholars (Emerson & Frosh, 2004; Gregg, 2006; Poindexter, 2003). It allows a broader range of narratives to be examined than does the approach of Labov (Riessman, 2008). Moreover, Gee's method may provide a fuller understanding of emotional experience than does that of Labov. (Indeed, Emerson and Frosh [2004] analyze the same text with both methods and come to that conclusion.)

The primary limitation of this method is that it does not attend to the interactional context in which a narrative is obtained or the wider societal discourses to which it may be linked, although Gee's current work focuses on the study of language in a broad social-cultural context (Gee, 2005). It is also cumbersome to use with lengthy transcriptions.

Gregg (2006) developed a method of textual analysis that allows an examination of a large amount of transcribed interview text, and it is to his method that I now turn.

ANALYSIS OF IDENTITY IN NARRATIVE

Gregg's interest is in identity and, in particular, how narrators construct identity in discourse. Thus, his interest is in both narrative and non-narrative forms of speech because he believes that individuals depend on both to fashion identities. His focus is on how individuals characterize themselves both explicitly and implicitly, arguing that implicit characterizations reflect important aspects of identity that may be ambiguous or contradictory or, perhaps, out of conscious awareness.

The approach is structural because there is an emphasis is on two structural elements of the text: the recurring contrasts the narrator makes or implies in relation to the self, others, and meaningful events and, secondly, how these contrasts are developed within a formulaic plot structure.

Definition of Narrative

Gregg treats narrative in terms of story and discourse in terms of narrative and propositional speech such as attitudes and beliefs.

Theoretical Orientation

Gregg's approach to identity is informed by the structuralist narratology of Lévi-Strauss (1975) and Propp (1928/1968). Although he does not adopt all of the assumptions regarding narrative of either scholar, he uses some of the concepts of each to understand how individuals craft an identity in discourse.

Specifically, he argues that "identity is organized simultaneously as (a) a deep structure underlying a set of homologous binary oppositions, as proposed by Lévi-Strauss (1975) in his studies of myth and (b) articulated in a *formulaic plot-episode structure*, as identified by Propp (1968) . . . (p. 64)."[2]

Central Question

Gregg describes his goal as proving that "identity self-representation requires a structural model (p. 66)." Thus, a central question in this form of analysis is: What is the narrator's identity?

Major Concepts

Gregg treats *identity* as multi-layered and as residing in the relationship between the surface and the deep structure of discourse. The *surface structure* of discourse of interest is the explicit and recurring contrasts the narrator makes in relation to self, meaningful events, and relationships. These explicit contrasts or *binary oppositions* serve as "self-definitional landmarks."

As the narrator shifts during speech between these explicit contrasts, Gregg argues he or she is conveying not only valuable information as to what is important but is also suggesting implicitly his or her identity. To clarify the identity to which these contrasts point, the investigator examines each explicit contrast and formulates what Gregg calls a *mediating term*. This term is not a midway point between the two opposing ideas that define each contrast but rather is a blend of the two that shares some, but not all, of the features of each pole.

Taken together, the binary oppositions and associated mediating terms point to an abstract *foundational binary opposition and associated mediating term* that constitutes the *deep structure* of discourse relating to the narrator's identity. This deep structure is elaborated within the sequence of episodes and plot structure of the broad story the narrator tells.

Orientation to Method

Gregg's (2006) analytic procedure, as outlined in his paper, *The Raw and the Bland: A Structural Model of Narrative Identity*, involves the following steps:

First, an interview is transcribed verbatim, and the material that is clearly irrelevant to the study's purpose is eliminated.

Second, following loosely the method of Gee (1991), the remaining material is parsed into stanzas, strophes, and parts.

Third, the explicit contrasts made in relation to the self, meaningful events and relationships within and across episodes are identified.

Fourth, the mediating term associated with each contrast is conceptualized.

Fifth, drawing on Propp's theory of the formulaic plot structure of folk tales, the parts of the transcribed interview are further defined in relation to the episode and plot structure of the story the narrator tells.

Sixth, the foundational binary opposition, which integrates at an abstract level all of the explicit contrasts or binary oppositions in the text, and an associated mediating term, is conceptualized and contextualized in relation to the episodic/plot structure.

The identity that emerges through such an analysis is defined therefore in relation to space, time, and story. Gregg summarizes: "It is defined by a paradigmatic 'surface structure' of homologous concrete contrasts that represent a deep abstract opposition, mediated by a third emergent category, which is developed by an implicit syntagmatic plot line (p. 83)."

ILLUSTRATION

Gregg describes the above model in the context of a case study he reports. The case was drawn from "Targets for the Worksite Prevention of Alcohol Abuse," a project of the United States National Institute on Alcohol Abuse and Alcoholism and the Robert Wood Johnson Foundation. The text is a transcription of an interview between a project interviewer and a vice president of a large company that develops industrial and aerospace plastics. The topic on which the interview focuses is the "corporate alcohol policies and programs in which his company and six others have agreed to participate (p. 65)."

The transcription of the entire text of the interview is available online (http://www.sesp.northwestern.edu/foley). Gregg eliminated material from the verbatim transcription that pertained to alcohol policies and other information that was not directly relevant to his interest in the narrator's identity.

Then, he parsed the remaining material into stanzas, strophes, and parts.

Box 5–4 contains strophes 1, 4, and 5 of part I (pp. 67–68). In this transcription, the bar [/] represents a break between lines.

The strophes begin to develop the contrast between engineers and blue-collar workers, the two groups that serve as "self-definitional" landmarks for the narrator. Strophes 1 and 4 describe the degreed engineers who dominate the company, emphasizing the professional demeanor the engineers maintain "at all times". Strophe 5 describes the difference in backgrounds between the company's engineers and managers recruited from the blue-collar workers who work in the company's plants. Strophe 5 also points to the alcohol problems that exist in these plants, especially in the South.

In stanza 9 of part I, a stanza that is not reproduced here, the narrator notes further that he doesn't mean that engineers don't drink, but he means that they "come from a climate where . . . doing book work in college was more important than hitting the frat house, or down at the corner bar (p. 68)." He then asserts elliptically, "That's not true of our sales force . . . (p. 68)."

Through close analysis of the remaining parts of the interview, parts entitled "On the road," "Dangers, challenges, tests," "The specter of alcohol abuse," "Treasures, tall tales, and war stories," and "Engineers all,"

Box 5–4

PART 1: ENGINEERS AND PEDDLERS

Strophe 1, stanza 5: Then, of course we have since dramatically moved away from that background/into having degreed engineers run this corporation./ In fact, I think one could say from a management perspective, without a fairly significant engineering degree,/ I think the prospects for somebody moving into very senior management, on the administrative side, are fairly remote.

Stanza 7: Although, I think, we've been successful, nevertheless they tend to regard their population as being extremely important on the technical side,/ both with degrees, particularly engineering degrees are certainly more honored/ if one were to go to a technical plant and say, 'Jeez, we have a problem. What do we need?'/ It's give me another process engineer or give me another project engineer.

Strophe 4, stanza 8: As a result, engineers are engineers. They tend to be, from an academic standpoint, more serious, certainly more analytical./ They are clearly individuals who are upper decile in terms of intelligence,/ and realistically portray themselves in a very professional manner at all times.

Strophe 5, stanza 10: As a result, I don't think you will see at the exempt level the alcohol issues that are present in other parts of the corporation./ On the non-exempt level [the hourly workers], I think if that happens, it would be traditionally [a matter of] where the plants are located./ Clearly we have a lot of plants in the South [where] there is the good old boy syndrome which I'm sure you're very familiar with./ It in fact exists out there.

Source: Gregg, G. (2006). The raw and the bland: A structural model of narrative identity. In D. McAdams, R. Josselson, & A. Lieblich (Eds), *Identity and story: Creating self in narrative* (pp. 63–87). Washington, DC: American Psychological Association.

Gregg observes that the explicit contrasts that permeate the meaningful events and relationships in the interview text continue to be contrasts between engineers and blue-collar workers with respect to their physical location, use of substances, character, and speech.

Gregg shows how these contrasts may be considered the surface manifestations of the narrator's representations—they sculpt the local culture of which he is apart; moreover, it is through these contrasts that the narrator defines implicitly a third group, sales people and crisis managers, of which he is a member, who function in a manner that differs somewhat from the other two groups.

The table below summarizes the explicit contrasts or binary oppositions that comprise the surface (paradigmatic) structure of the narrator's

	Paradigmatic Structure		
	Overcontrolled ◄—————————►		*Undercontrolled*
	Bland		*Raw*
Group:	degreed engineers	crisis managers & sales people	blue-collar workers
Location:	stay in [West Coast]	travel	stay out [South]
Substance:	none	alcohol	drugs and alcohol
Character:	nerds, boring	interesting, exciting high stress	uncouth, "pure fuel"
Speech:	uninteresting, silent [book work]	war stories, tall tales, treasures ↓ Control the out-of-control	confession, testimonial, [slang]

Source: Gregg, G. (2006). The raw and the bland: A structural model of narrative identity. In D. McAdams, R. Josselson, & A. Lieblich (Eds.), *Identity and story: Creating self in narrative* (pp. 63–87). Washington, DC: American Psychological Association.

representations and the foundational binary opposition (overcontrolled vs. undercontrolled) and the associated mediating term (control the out-of-control) that define its deep structure (Gregg, 2006, p. 79):

In relation to this analysis, Gregg notes:

> This is Lévi-Strauss's primitive thought par excellence: The deep structure of [the narrator's] . . . self-presentation consists of a binary opposition— whose concrete exemplars represent the abstractions "overcontrolled" (or bland) and "undercontrolled" (or raw), respectively- mediated by a third term: those who brave dangers to control the forces that tend to spin out of control (p. 81).

Thus, the narrator "drinks in a corner bar style and speaks with touches of working-class syntax and slang, but always retains control; he always keeps an eye fixed on the control panel but sallies forth to face forces of chaos the nerdy engineers keep under wraps (p. 83)." The foundational binary opposition and associated mediating term are further developed and contextualized within the framework of the story of the hero who leaves home and returns in triumph.

Gregg notes the narrator never provides a straightforward account of either his identity (or of drinking in his company), but the analysis shows "how things work in his universe." His "identity forms in the negative spaces of the cultural landscape he paints, and in this sense it is distributed throughout (Bruner, 1990) (Gregg, 2006, p. 84)."

USE

The method Gregg advances in the paper on which this section depends does not require fully formed stories for analysis to occur. Indeed, the investigator examines propositional speech and stories of events or of experience, and the method does not require the investigator to define exactly where a narrative, in a long stretch of text, begins and ends.

Moreover, the method allows for ambiguity or contradiction in identity to emerge, conditions that are not easily addressed in methods that emphasize explicit self-characterizations such as those employed by Lieblich and McAdams (*see* Chapter 4). Thus, Gregg's method is ideal for study of individuals whose identities may be difficult for them to claim or to explain or that may even be outside conscious awareness. I found the method well-suited, for example, for a study of the maternal identities of abusive and neglectful mothers who lost custody of their children (Wells, 2010).

CONCLUSION

This chapter has highlighted three approaches to the analysis of the structure of narratives: the analysis of sequence in narrative; the analysis of poetic structure of narrative; and the analysis of identity in narrative.

Through close analysis of how narrative is structured, these approaches allow nonobvious aspects of the meaning of narrative to emerge. The primary limitation of these methods is that they minimize the interactional and broader social context in which narrative is constructed and the import of both for its meaning. Discourse analysis, a topic to which I turn in the following two chapters, allows the investigator to consider these discourses in the analysis of narratives.

6

Application of Discursive Concepts to Analysis of Narratives

ANALYTIC FRAMEWORKS AND TWO IMPORTANT CONCEPTS

Discourse pertains to a broader range of talk and text than does narrative. In addition to narrative, discourse includes description, argumentation, evaluation, or reports. It is generally thought of as "broad patterns of language use"; however, within discourse analysis it has been specified further to include language use that is coherent and performs a social function (Coyle, 1995).

"[D]ifferent traditions called 'discourse analysis' have emerged in different disciplinary environments. Often these traditions are structured by and against, the basic issues of the parent discipline (Hepburn & Potter, 2007, pp. 168–169)." For example, within linguistics, discourse analysis has focused on how sentences combine to form discourse; in cognitive psychology, it has focused on how mental schemas are used to make sense of narrative; within social psychology, it has focused on how discourse constructs reality; and within post-structuralism, it has focused on how discourse constitutes objects and subjects (Potter, 2004)

I focus here on the later two approaches because they hold the greatest potential for investigation of social-psychological phenomenon of interest to social work. Some analysts are interested in how individuals use words to construct their reality and to manage their stakes in conversation, whereas others are interested in how individuals draw on discourses that are widely available in society that shape what is possible for them to think and to feel (Willig, 2003). Thus, discourse analysts are concerned with not only how individuals produce discourse but also how they are products of discourse (Edley, 2001).[1]

Some of the concepts of discourse analysis have been incorporated into forms of narrative analysis, specifically critical narrative analysis (Emerson & Frosh, 2004), and discourse-analytic concepts have been applied to the analysis of narratives (Hall, Slembrouck, & Sarangi, 2006; Hydén & Överlien, 2004; Sands, 2004). Discourse-analytic concepts are especially relevant to an examination of social work practice because social work depends on talk, and their use may clarify taken-for-granted practices and open them to discussion and debate (White, 2001).

White (2001), for example, studied how social workers transformed and subverted parents' accounts of life with children who were difficult into accounts of parents who were incompetent. This transformation was accomplished by selecting and ordering ambiguous information into a coherent story. She found that in the telling, the story attained the status of fact; worked to blame parents; silenced other readings of the case; and reproduced, perhaps unwittingly, a prevailing cultural discourse, "the parent as culpable discourse", that emphasizes the importance of nurture over nature in relation to children's successful development.

It is useful to summarize two broad approaches to discourse analysis, Discursive Psychology (DP) and Foucauldian Discourse Analysis (FDA) (Willig, 2003), in order to illustrate the discourse concepts that have been widely applied in the analysis of narratives and to lift up their potential for language-based research on social work-related problems and practice.

ANALYTIC FRAMEWORK: DISCURSIVE PSYCHOLOGY

Definitions

Discursive psychology is a broad perspective on psychology that emphasizes performance or how individuals use talk to accomplish certain actions (Potter, 2003). It grew out of discourse analysis as it developed in social psychology (Wiggins & Potter, 2008). It focuses on how individuals represent objects and subjects and with what effects for self and others. Discursive psychology has contributed to the reconceptualization of foundational concepts in psychology such as the self, for example, in terms of talk rather than in terms of traits, roles, or "pre-existent natures" (Potter& Wetherell, 1987).

Theoretical Orientation

Discursive psychology is based on three primary assumptions (Wiggins & Potter, 2008): One, discourse is comprised of language such as words, categories, and idioms and that these constructions constitute social reality. Thus, talk produces social reality. Two, discourse is "action-oriented"; talking and writing has a point—that is, to explain, justify, invite, or blame. Thus, talk and action cannot be separated. Three, discourse is located sequentially, institutionally, and rhetorically.

Potter (2003) illustrates this third point when he shows how a call from a young woman to a child abuse hotline is located within the context of the conversation between the individual making and the individual answering the call; it is located within conventions for talk on a telephone hotline, and it is located rhetorically in that the caller describes herself as "a very close friend" of the abused in order to persuade the other that she is a sympathetic and perhaps knowledgeable informant.

Discursive psychology draws heavily on constructivism, the view that talk and text construct social reality rather than reflect social reality (*see* the *Journal of Constructivist Psychology* for further discussion of this movement), social constructionism, the view that the meaning of words depends on their utility in social relationships (Gergen, 2009), and conversation analysis (Pomerantz, 1984, cited in Wiggins & Potter, 2008).

Central Question

Central questions in this approach focus on how something is accomplished through discourse, or questions such as these: How do individuals manage their interests in conversations within specific interpersonal contexts? How is talk organized to make a claim or to undermine an alternative presumption? (Willig, 2003)

Major Concepts

Analysts examine language closely through attention to terminology, metaphors, and other figures of speech to identify how individuals construct subjects and objects and construe their stakes in conversations. Thus, key sensitizing concepts include *subject, objects,* and *the management of stakes in conversations.*

Orientation to Method

Discourse analysts prefer to study naturally-occurring conversations and texts; however, interview-based data have also been examined. In either case, the analyst employs audio-recordings of talk and transcriptions of talk and investigates how discourse is organized to understand what it is doing. Discursive psychology relies on Jefferson's system of transcription that was developed for conversation analysis (Jefferson, 2004). This system emphasizes aspects of interpersonal interaction, such as intonation, that participants use to make sense of conversations. Potter (2003) argues that transcriptions should be used in conjunction with audio-recordings in the analysis of data.

Discursive psychology is defined more by its focus and assumptions than by its method (Wiggins & Potter, 2008). It focuses initially on a broad topic, and through the process of data collection, specific research questions are then identified. Data are collected with an eye toward building a sufficient dataset from which to test interpretations. A corpus of data may be built by collecting data from, for example, the same individual over time, across individuals, or across settings with the same function. It is important to collect a sufficiently large database that it includes standard and exceptional patterns. Analysis depends on multiple readings of transcripts, identifying portions that are relevant to the research questions, examining how individuals construct objects, subjects, and manage their stakes in conversations across contexts and with what consequences (Willig, 2003).

Specific analytic advice has been provided by Antaki, Billig, Edwards, and Potter (2003) (cited in Wiggins & Potter, 2008); Potter and Wetherell (1987), and Potter (2003). Potter (2003) highlights the importance of turn-taking, noting that "Any turn of talk is oriented to what came before, and sets up an environment for what comes next. . . . Close attention to this turn-by-turn display of understanding provides one important check (p. 85)" on interpretation and draws on analytic techniques developed successfully in conversation analysis.

ILLUSTRATION

Willig (2003) highlights the study of Wiggins, Potter, and Wildsmith (2001) as an illustration of this mode of discourse analysis. In their investigation, three families recorded all mealtime conversations over a 7-day period. In this report, transcripts of audio-recordings of one family's discussions about food during mealtimes were analyzed. One stretch of talk between Sue, the mother in the family, and her two daughters, Chloe and Emily (shown in Box 6–1), illustrates how food *is constructed as an object* through dialogue.

In this text, a dot enclosed in parentheses [(.)] indicates a pause of less than two-tenths of a second; a number enclosed in parentheses refers to the number of pauses in tenths of a second; a letter or word that is underlined indicates a sound that is emphasized; and a colon (:) indicates extension of the proceeding vowel sound.

The authors emphasize several points in relation to this brief exchange: individuals are involved with each other's consumption of food; eating is an activity for which individuals are held accountable; and Chloe constructs the food as "foul," thereby providing an explanation as to why she is not eating. Each "turn of talk" may provide a

---

Box 6–1

1. Sue: Come on there was only a tiny bit of (.) of
2.   <u>salm</u>on just e:at <u>salm</u>on
3. Chloe: N:<u>o</u> its <u>fo:ul</u>
4.   (2.0)
5. Emily: I've eaten mine
6. Sue: Ye:ah you've eaten y<u>ours</u>
7.   (1.0)
8. Chloe: I've been <u>try</u>ing but mine's inedible

Source: Wiggins, S., Potter, J., & Wildsmith, A. (2001). Eating your words: discursive psychology and the reconstruction of eating practices. *Journal of Health Psychology*, 6(1), 5–15.

new construction, for example, Emily asserts the food is edible and the problem then becomes Chloe's reaction to food and not the food itself.

The authors note "previous studies have tended to treat food as an object to be individually appraised, and responded to-through eating it, or not eating it . . . [w]hat has been overlooked [in experimental methods] is the fluidity and scope of food construction (Wiggins, Potter, & Wildsmith, 2001, p. 9)." Through this work, food is highlighted as a social activity in which descriptions of "food, body shape and activities . . . can be used to accomplish a range of tasks (refusing and accepting, accounting for appetite and so on) (p. 13)."

They address the implicit question as to the use of DP, when they note: "It is certainly the case that discursive psychology is avoiding the factors and effects model that is typical elsewhere in psychology . . . However, the attention to people's situated actions is attention to *their* issues of motivation and accountability (p. 13)." This has clear implications for interventions designed to alter food construction within families to promote healthier relationships and patterns of food consumption.

A second study illuminates *how individuals protect their stakes in conversations* (Potter, 2004). This report focuses on a therapy session in which the husband, Jimmy, complains of the flirtatious behavior of his wife, Connie, with other men, and Connie suggests her husband is pathologically jealous. Potter shows how the husband uses the phrase, "*I don't know*," to manage his stake in the conversation that is shown in Box 6–2.

Potter notes that Jimmy's description of his wife's skirt length is critical here because it relates to why they are in therapy and who has the problem that may need fixing. Because the description of the skirt length could point to Jimmy's wife's inappropriate behavior *or* to Jimmy's obsessive recall of his wife's appearance, Potter hypothesizes that Jimmy inserts the phrase, "I don't know," in line 16, immediately after his description of the length of his wife's skirt to ward off the latter interpretation.

In this text, a dot enclosed by parentheses [(.)] indicates a pause of less than two-tenths of a second; a number enclosed in parentheses indicates the number of pauses in tenths of a second; a letter or word that is underlined indicates a sound that is emphasized; and a colon (:) indicates extension of the proceeding vowel sound.

Box 6–2

1. Jimmy: A:nd (0.8) we <u>sat</u> in the pub and
2. we (.) <u>star</u>ted to discuss
3. we had a <u>l</u>ittle bit of a <u>row</u>. (2.0)
4. In the pub.(0.6)
5. And <u>a</u>rguing about the time. (0.8)
6. U:m (.) whe:n these people came in.(.)
7. It was: (.) John and Caroline.(1.0)
8. And they they <u>had</u>–(.)
9. this <u>oth</u>er fella <u>D</u>ave.
10. With them as well
    [6 lines omitted in the original]
11. they <u>all</u> came in the pub anyway. (1.0)
    [3 lines omitted]
12. They <u>sat</u> in–on the <u>o</u>ther side.
13. (1.0)
    [16 lines omitted in original]
14. And uh:: (1.0)
15. Connie had a short skirt on
16. I don't know.(1.0)
17. And I kn<u>ew</u> this- (0.6)
18. uh ah- maybe I <u>had</u> met him.(1.0) Ye:h (.)
19. I musta met Da:ve before. (0.8)
20. But I'd <u>heard</u> he was a bit of a la:d.
21. He <u>did</u>n't care: (1.0) <u>who</u> he (0.2) chatted up or (.)

Source: Potter, J. (2004). Discourse analysis as a way of analyzing naturally occurring talk. In D. Silverman (Ed.), *Qualitative research: Theory, method and practice* (2nd ed.) (pp. 200–221). London: Sage.

Shortly after Jimmy's long narrative, Connie, interjects:

Connie: My skirt <u>prob</u>ably went up to about there. ((gestures))
Jimmy: ((a sharp intake of breath))
Connie: <u>May</u>be a bit <u>short</u>er. It was <u>done</u> for <u>no</u>- I never <u>look</u>ed at that
         particular bloke when I did it it was my friend commented Oh
         you're <u>show</u>ing o:ff a lot o' leg tonight (Potter, 2004, p.214).

This stretch of talk shows that Jimmy and his wife are both quite sure of the length of her skirt, and it advances Potter's hypothesis that Jimmy uses the phrase "*I don't know*" to make a claim as to the nature of their marital problem rather than to state his confusion.

Thus, Discursive psychology helps to illuminate the stakes that individuals have in conversations and holds the potential, therefore, to clarify the focus for interventions to help individuals to realize their aims.

ANALYTIC FRAMEWORK: FOUCAULDIAN DISCOURSE ANALYSIS

Definitions and Theoretical Orientation

Foucauldian discourse analysis draws on the work of the French philosopher, Foucault. His work concerned how systems of thought, or discursive formations, determine the boundaries of *what may be thought* in a given domain and in a given period (Stanford Encyclopedia of Philosophy Online, Michel Foucault, Sections 3.0-3.4, 2008). He argued these systems are governed by rules that operate beneath consciousness. Changes from one system to another depended on "contingent turns of history" rather than inevitable historical trends. Both stability and transition in thought may be uncovered through an historical method, with the analyst continuing to examine materials until he or she identifies where and how concepts originated, stabilized, and or changed over time. He contended that modern systems of thought, especially modern bodies of social or scientific knowledge, are closely connected to modern structures of power such that control over individuals is exerted as a function of being an object of study, of being an object of scrutiny by others, and by internalizing norms so that individuals become "self-scrutinizing and self-forming *subjects.*"

Discourse analysis that is informed by his work is interested in how these systems of thought "facilitate and limit, engage and constrain what can be said, by whom, where and when (Willig, 2003, p. 171, citing Parker, 1992)." Foucauldian discourse analysis does not fit well into a social scientific paradigm that seeks to accumulate decontextualized statements of knowledge, in part because it treats truth as an historical rather than an epistemological concept (Arribas-Allyon & Walkerdine, 2007).

One focus of this approach is how power works through prevailing discourse so that some may be silenced and others may find voice

(Tamboukou, 2008). In this respect, its aim is similar to that of critical discourse analysis.[2]

Discourse in this tradition does not refer to talk or to text, although analysts study both, but rather to a body of knowledge—a discipline and the practices through which objects (ideas) within that discipline are formed (Arribas-Allyon & Walkerdine, 2008). Foucault, for example, examined the conditions "of possibility for the emergence of knowledges, practices, objects, and programmes, etc" in relation to the idea that sexual practices define the modern self (Kendall & Wickham, 2007, p. 132). As a result, in this tradition the word, *discourse*, is sometimes capitalized in order to distinguish this use of the term from other more widely used definitions.

Major Concepts

Some key concepts in Foucauldian discourse analysis (FDA) are *subject positions*, a "location for persons within a structure of rights and duties for those who use that repetoire" (Davies & Harré, 1999, p. 35); *subjectification*, or on what authority and through what practices individuals regulate themselves; and *technologies*, primarily technologies of self (systems of thought and actions that individuals use to regulate their actions) and technologies of power (an assemblage of knowledge, people, space, for example, that act on individuals from without) (Arribas-Allyon & Walkerdine, 2008).

However, there is not one approach to FDA. Some scholars adopt Foucault's emphasis on identifying the conditions under which an object is formed within a discourse through a rigorous examination of the relevant historical record of texts (Kendall & Wickham, 2008); others take a more ahistorical approach and focus on how individuals are positioned by discourses and the consequences of these positions for subjectivity (Willig, 2003).

A central difference between DP and FDA of either type is that DP emphasizes how individuals actively use discourse to construct objects and subjects ("the thinking self, the I") (Stanford Encyclopedia of Philosophy Online, 2008, Section 4.3), whereas FDA emphasizes how discourse makes certain positions and ways of being available to individuals (Willig, 2003).

Central Question

The organizing question is: "How does something come to exist?" (Kendall & Wickham, 2008, p.132). An important secondary question is "How does discourse construct subjects and objects?" (Willig, 2003, p. 172).

Orientation to Method

There is not one methodological approach to FDA, in part because of differences in use of historical material. Methodological guidelines have been developed by Arribas-Allyon and Walkerdine (2008), Kendall and Wickham (1999), Parker (1992), and Willig (2003).

Across methods, however, there is an emphasis on an examination of how discursive objects are constructed within a discourse (based on an examination of a corpus of statements drawn from political, expert, and autobiographical texts, social practices, and social interactions) (Arribas-Allyon & Walkerdine, 2008); an examination of the subject positions within the discourse and the ways in which they shape opportunities for action; and an examination of subjective experience within those positions).

Thus, FDA does not take a linguistic approach to analysis of discourse.

Illustration

Arribas-Allyson and Walkerdine (2008) highlight an example of FDA from Arribas-Allyson's study of welfare "rationalities" and "the effects these have on practices of freedom and self-formation (p. 103)." Focusing on Australia, this study examined the discourses that made the problem considered in need of solution in the 1990s—welfare dependency— "thinkable." The first goal was achieved through the location of the origin of contemporary Australian welfare policy in 19th century social policies that established the Australian welfare state, especially laws designed to distinguish the deserving from the undeserving poor.

The second goal of the study was achieved through examination of the discourse of current recipients of welfare. The authors quote one of the participants, Angela, a young woman who lived in a rural area with high unemployment, to illustrate their analytic approach. Box 6–3 contains relevant text from the interview with her.

Box 6–3

I think that there is a lot more choices elsewhere, like when I moved back from Sydney and I said to mum, "I am never going to work in a super-market, I am not going to do this and I am not going to do that," and then after about a year I asked mum, "I wonder if they have got any jobs at the checkout" . . . (in original) I don't know it is just the situation I am in and I am not happy and I am starting to realize that you can't be too choosy . . . then, um the fact that I am open minded about it all rather than "I am only going to do this," especially in town where there are not that many oppor-tunities, . . . but I mean like if I really wanted to I could get up and leave, I mean I have done it before on less than what I've got now . . . but like really I have got nothing holding me back, I can go and do whatever I want.

Source: Arribas-Ayllon, M. & Walkerdine, V. (2008). Foucauldian discourse analysis. In C. Willig & W. Stainton-Rogers (Eds), *The Sage handbook of qualitative research in psychology* (pp. 91–108). London: Sage.

In their analysis of this stretch of text, Arribas-Ayllon and Walkerdine (2008) note that the *subject position* of welfare recipient:

> threatens to subsume the more virtuous position of . . . "jobseeker," in which case Angela must present herself as having undergone some kind of personal and moral transformation. What is also interesting is the particular "technology" from which the affirmative voice draws. In the absence of any real change in the material circumstances of the commu-nity, it is primarily a psychological relation to self that emerges as a new valuation of work: the . . . checkout job is transposed into a lucrative possibility, not because material circumstances demand *any* form of paid work, but because "self-realization" is a more praiseworthy way of articulating self-reliance. In order to evade the stigma of dependency, Angela draws on a "psychological" technology of self-improvement to position herself in alignment with a moral order (p. 104).

They continue that what recedes into the background of her account is that this discourse of *subjectification* cannot address the "insecurity of work"; that it transposes economic and political contradictions into "personal difficulties"; and that the position, welfare recipient, presup-poses an ethical failure and, under conditions of welfare reform, requires an "ethical reconstruction of the self" producing self-blame and ambivalence among recipients.

They conclude that Angela's experience, including her fantasy of unlimited choice, may be more clearly understood when placed within the historical context that they provide.

Thus, FDA helps the analyst to articulate alternative ways of understanding what is taken as necessary or as self-evident in a given domain. As a result, Foucauldian-inspired investigations could be used to suggest how problems could be reconceptualized to promote genuine empowerment among the powerless.

TWO DISCURSIVE CONCEPTS AND ANALYSIS OF NARRATIVES

Of the concepts used in the discourse analytic frameworks described above, I highlight two—*position and voice*—because they have been used widely in the analysis of narratives.

Position

Positioning "theory" (Harré & Van Langenhove, 1999), an influential perspective and set of concepts with which to view social life, proposes that most social psychological phenomena are discursively produced within local contexts, and as a result, psychology should be the study of everyday discourse.

Central concepts within this theoretical framework include position and positioning. *Position* refers to a speaker's moral and personal attributes that shape how what is said may be understood. These attributes are linked to culturally recognizable storylines. *Positioning* refers to communicative strategies used to assign the self or others to positions. In research, positioning has been conceptualized in relation to:

> [R]elationships between the speaker and what is being said . . . ; through relationships between self and other, or speaker and hearer, in face-to-face occasions of talk and interaction; through relationships represented in the propositional content of talk (what is one textual character doing to another textual character?); through relationships to the dominant ideologies, widespread social practices and underlying power structures

drawn together as Discourse (Gee, 1996) (De Fina, Schiffrin, & Bamberg, 2006b, p. 7).

De Fina, Schiffrin, and Bamberg (2006b) summarize methods used to examine how narrators position themselves in studies of identity, and these include comparing a current and a former self; assigning others to social categories; aligning the self, directly or indirectly, vis-à-vis others; and adopting a stance toward discourses, writ large. Thus, the concept, *position*, when compared to the concept, *role*, is best understood as an interactional concept (Ribeiro, 2006). Wortham (2000, 2001) suggests additional tools with which to examine positioning.

The Hydén and Överlien (2004) study of counselors' dilemmas treating sexually abused girls provides one example of how these concepts are used to analyze narratives: In the stretch of talk in Box 6–4, Överlien (labeled C. O. in the text) and one of the study participants (a male counselor who is labeled P) discuss the counselor's experience of placing a girl in solitary confinement against her will (Hydén & Överlien, 2004, pp. 261–262). In this text, a dot enclosed in parentheses (.) refers to a pause of less than two-tenths of a second.

In turn 5, the counselor, through the use of the term, *us*, simultaneously positions himself as one of a group of male counselors, and redirects the blame for the situation from himself to, perhaps, the group as a whole. In turn 13, the counselor, by shifting from the use of the word, *you*, to the word, *I*, and then back to the word, *you*, also positions himself, as although inexperienced, as not being alone in having this sort of encounter.

The authors highlight how when an adolescent girl re-lives the story of abuse, it has the power to position new people within an old story without their awareness. They show, with the concept of positioning, how the male resident counselor does not blame his victimization on either the adolescent or himself but on her life story. Thus, she is not a perpetrator and he is not a victim.

Through a nuanced analysis of several stories and the ethnographic data they had also collected, the clinical complexities of this sort of work and the programmatic challenges that must be met were revealed. The authors concluded:

> The outcome was quite disheartening. The staff were supposed to be active agents in the highly valued construction of a sexual abuse story

---

Box 6–4

1. P.: we had a girl here before who got taken to court because she kept on threatening so much (.) she'd been terribly abused that (.) was the worst thing I've been through she'd been (pause) I she's I don't know what she's doing now but she was sentenced to inpatient psychiatric care but she had been (.) raped by her brothers and guys and all kinds of people ever since she was like little

2. C.Ö.: Mm

3. P.: and we just keep constantly having to put her in solitary and solitary and solitary

4. C.Ö.: Mm

5. P.: it was as if she went on repeating the things she had gone through by making us men you know (.) lie down on her and

6. C.Ö.: Mm

7. P.: hold her and (.) that kind of thing

8. C.Ö.: Mm

9. P.: it was kind of creepy

10. C.Ö.: Yes

11. P.: Really

12. C.Ö.: I'm sure

13. P.: Yeah (.) but you don't realize it until it's (.) I was pretty new then and you didn't realize until you got some distance to it that she was reexperiencing those things.

Source: Hydén, M. & Overlien, C. (2004). "Doing" narrative analysis. In D. Padgett (Ed.), *The qualitative research experience* (pp. 250–268). Belmont, CA: Thomson Brooks/Cole.

---

that could form the basis for healing the wounds the traumatic events had caused. The main plot in story after story they gave us referenced how they were exceeded by narrative power and positioned powerless to such an extent that their work identity was at stake (pp. 266–267).

Voice

A concept drawn from literary theory that is related to that of positioning is that of voice (Bakhtin, 1981; Dentith, 1995). Bakhtin, a literary theorist, developed a theory of voice, primarily in relation to his analyses of Dostoyevsky's novels (Wiley, 2009 citing Bakhtin, 1984), which has been influential in discourse and narrative studies. He advanced the idea that characters have a "voice" but that each one is "multi-vocal, polyphonous and replete with sub-voices (Wiley, 2009, p. 4)." There may be a central voice with variations, some of which may be "barely audible" or even suppressed. For Bakhtin, voice implies dialogue, a conversation with the "other" or with the "self" in the form of "inner speech". In the latter case, dialogues may be with institutions as well as with the self. Wiley observes that Bakhtin "finds voices in social forces, the surrounding community and historical currents. Any social element that has a meaning also has a message, and this message can be decoded into a voice (p. 4)."

Within the social sciences, the concept of voice has been used to identify characters who are similar to social types and to shared knowledge of these types (Sands, 2004; Wortham, 2001) and to prevailing ideologies associated with institutions (Bell, 2006).

Bell (2006) illustrates the latter use of voice. She examined the identity of one woman through a close analysis of her story of becoming a mother. The woman had been exposed prenatally to a synthetic estrogen that is now known to cause cancer and fertility problems in women. She had given birth to a child with severe abnormalities, and she had had several miscarriages.

Bell observes how the stretch of talk in Box 6–5 shows how the narrator calls on the voice of medical science ("I *should* be able to carry, a baby to term.") and positions herself as a patient ("They wanted to see if I had a double *uterus*."). In this text, emphasis is indicated by italics and pauses are noted by commas.

The narrator continues the story with graphic details as to the medical tests that she had and then references the experiences of her first child in the hospital: "I had spent a lot of time in [a hospital with Grace]/I had seen a lot of really gruesome things, (inhale)" (p. 242), although the details of her ill daughter's experiences are never revealed. Bell observes that the failure of the narrator to speak about her daughter's body, in contrast to the vivid detail that she provides regarding her own, is a way of "wielding silence." Her silence in the interview, moreover, replicates the silence she showed medical professionals. She inhibited her own reactions in order to be the mother she wanted to be for her child. Thus, it can be seen that *voice* may also be considered in relation to *silence*.

The narrator's silence is also one aspect of the way in which she tells or *performs* her story. Goffman (1959) used the concept of performance to conceptualize ways in which social actors perform preferred identities,

Box 6–5

(s) They wanted to see if
(t) I had a double *uterus*
(u) or if it was you know "T" shaped
(v) that I couldn't *carry* a *baby* (inhale),
(w) (voice getting softer) you know cause my my first daughter was prema*ture*
(x) and now this baby, which appeared normal
(y) um uh miscarried (tch),
(z) (voice gets louder again) they found that
(aa) I did have an unusual shaped uterus
(bb) but it wasn't *severely* malformed . . .
(ff) you know that I *should* be able to carry, a baby to term (inhale)

Source: Bell, S. (2006). Intensive mothering in spite of it all. In A. De Fina, D. Schiffrin, & M. Bamberg (Eds), *Discourse and identity* (pp. 233–251). Cambridge: Cambridge University Press.

especially in situations in which they wish to save face. Focusing on narrative as performance, Langellier (2001) distinguishes between aspects of storytelling that enhance the experience of telling or listening to a story, aspects such as the providing vivid detail or the use of gestures, and the ways in which storytelling shapes or even destabilizes the identities of storyteller and audience. For example, the narrator in Bell's study may be shaping not only her identity as a woman defined by mothering but she may also be countering feminist views of mothering she believed were held by Bell.

USE

As this chapter has shown, although discourse-analytic concepts are linked to a diverse set of disciplines and theoretical traditions, the two adopted widely within psychology, Discursive psychology and Foucauldian discourse analysis, hold particular promise for studies of problems of concern to social work.

Indeed, some investigators use concepts drawn from both traditions. For example, Gillies' (1999) analysis of the meaning of cigarette smoking among working class women in the United Kingdom identified constructions women used to explain smoking, such as *smoking is a loss of self-control,* and societal discourses, such as *smoking is an addiction,* through which women smokers were positioned as helpless.

Based on her findings, Gillies posited an alternative view that could provide the basis of new interventions to facilitate change:

> Rather than viewing the body as a dominant, controlling force, as in a discourse of addiction, or as a separate entity in need of regulation and repression, as in a construction of self-control, a more affirmative construction would emphasize pleasure, strength and vitality . . . [and the promotion of other] forms of physical enjoyment (p. 84).

Her conclusion realizes one goal of discourse analysis—to create a space in which to imagine other ways in which life may be lived.

CONCLUSION

This chapter has highlighted two discourse-analytic frameworks, Discursive psychology and Foucauldian discourse analysis. Both approaches hold promise for social scientific investigations that focus on interactions between and among social workers and their clients and individuals with whom social work has traditionally been engaged.

Both analytic frameworks have limitations, however. Discursive psychology tends to attend to text and to ignore the way in which the story to which a text refers has been co-constructed or performed (Roberts, 2002). Investigators using Foucauldian discourse analysis tend to attend to the historical-social-political context in which texts are produced and to ignore what individuals are actually saying (Roberts, 2002).

Indeed, Roberts (2002) suggests that both forms of analysis are inherently incompatible with narrative in that the latter depends on story, plot, and time, and assumes an agentic actor capable of narrative construction, and the former does not. Arribas-Allyon and Walkerdine (2008) counter, however, that in discourse analysis, human agency is not abandoned but rather is "placed at the limits of thought" (Arribas-Allyon & Walkerdine, 2008, p. 106). Thus, discourse always implies *counter-discourses* and the possibility of resistance.

However incompatible assumptions under-girding discourse-analytic frameworks and narrative may be, concepts drawn from discourse analysis such as position and voice have been used productively in narrative analysis, and they have been integrated into emerging traditions of narrative analysis to which I turn in Chapter 7.

7

Analysis of Narrative in Context

INTEGRATIVE APPROACHES

Methods of narrative analysis are evolving. Efforts are being made to incorporate concepts drawn from discourse analysis, such as those described above, into existing approaches and to consider how narrative, the occasion of its telling, and the wider societal discourses of which it may be a part are inter-related. I highlight here the work of three scholars, Emerson and Frosh (2004) and Squire (2007a), whose work expands the repertoire of approaches to narrative study. Because the investigations of which their methodological innovations are a part are complex, I advise readers to read the authors' volumes to which I refer in their entirety.

CRITICAL NARRATIVE ANALYSIS

Emerson and Frosh (2004) published a volume, *Critical Narrative Analysis: A Guide to Practice*, in which they examined narrative texts from a sexually abusive boy with an approach they label *critical narrative analysis*. In this approach, texts are analyzed in a series of steps, moving from a micro- to a macro-level of analysis. Through this process, the authors conceptualize how the boy constructs the account of his life in his family and his abusive behavior, and then they articulate implications of their analysis for clinical work with him and other sexually abusive boys.

Definition of Narrative

Emerson and Frosh (2004) define narrative as a relatively coherent personal story, with a beginning, middle, and an end, that is co-constructed by an interviewee and interviewer in relation to foci on which an investigation is to focus.

Although they acknowledge the utility of Labov's definition of narrative and what he calls "core narratives" in a text (*see* Chapter 5 of this volume), they emphasize that narratives may be embedded in long stretches of talk between an interviewer and interviewee and enveloped in broad themes that characterize an entire interview that are important to their understanding.

Theoretical Orientation

They locate their work within three scholarly traditions: the field of psychosocial studies, constructionist theory, and psycho-analytic theory. Psychosocial studies is a field within psychology in which the individual and society are conceptualized as "entwined" (Frosh, 2003). The emphasis is the study of individuals within the context of a specific personal and social location and set of concerns.

Constructionist theory (McNamee & Gergen, 1992) is concerned with how individuals construct rather than represent reality through talk.

Psycho-analytic theory and practice emphasize the role of the unconscious, intrapsychic conflict, and mechanisms of defense, among other things. The authors' application of this perspective to narrative work underscores the importance of interruptions in narrative. They argue that interruptions may point to the narrator's effort to make sense, in the moment, of the story being told and to a breakdown in the narrator's routine speech in "the face of pressing unconscious material (Frosh & Young, in press)."

Central Question

Within this framework, central questions include questions such as these: How does this person, in this context, come to give the account he does?

How is it constituted? What psychological processes are at work in it? What does it do?

Orientation to Method

Drawing on ideas central to both narrative analysis and discourse analysis, the authors advance their approach as a method through which one may understand, in particular, how individuals construct personal narratives in situations in which there are disconnections between them and the social contexts of which they are a part.

The method involves five broad steps: audio-recording and transcribing verbatim an interview; separating the narrative from the non-narrative text, guided by Labov's definitional criteria (Labov, 1972; *see* Chapter 5 of this volume); conducting an initial analysis of the broad themes of the entire text; selecting and analyzing a small number of narratives that are well-elaborated and of the greatest theoretical interest, relying on the approach of Gee (1991; *see* Chapter 5 of this volume), adapted to include the role of the interviewer (Mishler, 1997; Riessman, 1993); and examining the transcribed narratives in relation to the interpersonal context in which they were generated, the broad themes that characterize the entire interview, and the societal discourses that may be informing the exchange. (They provide a useful comparison and contrast of the approach of Labov and Gee by analyzing the same narrative with each approach.)

Major Concepts and Illustration

The authors illustrate their approach with one case, a boy identified as Lance who sexually abused other boys. Working with a transcript from two interviews with Lance, they examine questions such as these:

> [H]ow does a sexually abusive boy make sense of his sexually abusive behaviors? How does he see his sense of self, of masculinity, of others and of relationships? On what bases and through what processes does he make choices leading to and maintaining the sexual abuse of other children? How can the interpenetration of this boy's personal narratives and canonical (i.e. widely shared) cultural discourses be read so that agency and accountability neither dissolve into radical relativism nor remain merely individualistic and pathologised, uncritically examined in the legal, treatment and media frameworks of dominant narratives? (p. 11).

In short: How may the boy's narratives best be understood in order to expand our understanding of how he best may be helped?

The analysis of narratives selected for intensive analysis builds on the data-analytic questions posed by Gee (1991). These questions are hierarchical in that the narrative analyst's answer to one question is anchored in details of the answer(s) to prior questions (Emerson & Frosh, 2004, p. 77). The primary questions the analyst addresses are italicized in the paragraphs below, and they are placed in the order in which they are to be examined.

How is narrative text organized as speech? To address this question, the authors parse a narrative that has been transcribed verbatim, following Gee (1991), into pitch glides, idea units, lines, stanzas, strophes, and parts, including the interviewer's words.

This organization is essential to addressing the remaining questions. In particular, it helps the authors to consider how the narrative fits into the broad themes that characterize the entire interview in which it is embedded and the ways in which those themes may reflect canonical narratives.

For example, the authors examine one narrative in relation to the interviewer's efforts to formulate a core question that he wants Lance to address: "How is it that they find you doing that [sexually abusing other boys] even when you're saying that it's wrong?" The authors first parse the narrative that was elicited by this question into pitch glides, idea units, lines, stanzas, strophes, and parts. They then consider the narrative in relation to a broad theme of "desire" that characterizes the entire interview and the societal discourse to which that theme is linked: the societal discourse that treats masculine desire as irrepressible.

Why have speakers made this particular connection at this point? This question refers to how a connection makes sense within the logic of the parts and the whole of the interview. It refers to how language is used to achieve cohesion across the parts of a narrative and the entire interview in which it is embedded.

For example, the authors observe, in relation to Lance's comment that "I LOVE solving/other people's PROBLEMS; but I HATE/having to SOLVE my OWN":

> may contain a significant ambivalence, muted both by the unemphasized "but" and by the parallel pitch glide foci of love/hate, an ambivalence about whether Lance would "LOVE" to be able to solve his "OWN" problems like he implies he is able to solve "other people's" or whether

Lance's focus on other people's problems supports a strategy to avoid or resist what he hates—having to solve his own problems (p. 58).

The authors then show how this comment and comments made later in the interview may be most fully understood in relation to the broad theme of *how Lance might learn to solve his own problems as a boy in his family* that cross-cut the interview.

What is the plot and its significance? This question refers to how the narrator uses language to tell a story and to illustrate the story's main point.

For example, the authors examine one narrative produced in response to the interviewer's question, "What would you say you've learned about being a boy/by growing up in your home?" Through an analysis of the text, the authors show how the narrator not only tells a story of how the females in his family get what they want but they also show, through the narrator's act of comparing himself with other members of his family, the emotional salience to him of the point that he is making.

Who or what is the subject of a stanza? This question refers to how the narrator uses psychological subjects, or the "subject positions or points of view from which the material in a stanza is viewed (p. 70)", in his speech. They investigate the subjects used, whether they change, and whether or not there are patterns in the changes made.

For example, through a complex and nuanced analysis of the narrator's use of the words *I, we, he, she, it, and women*, the authors suggest Lance's shifts in use of these subjects point to the importance of his father's absence on the family, and Lance's "uncertainty about how he and his wants are situated in relation to them (p. 73)."

Why is the focus so important? This last question refers to the foci of idea units. The authors consider why foci are important within and across the stanzas of a text. For example, the authors show how Lance "exonerates" his mother from "having power over his father, but then seems more satisfied with the explanation of her having power in the form of being 'stubborn' (p. 75)." The exoneration, however, hinges on his father's absence from home due to his work.

The authors extend the close textual analysis of narratives contained within an interview with a second level of thematic analysis across the entire interview text that allows them to theorize that Lance links masculinity to exertion of power, but discounts and rejects, with some ambivalence, accountability as feminine. They then link themes such as this one to broader cultural discourses pertaining to masculinity in which they are embedded. They conclude:

> Nevertheless, the story of his ascribed problematic identity . . . is not only overtly linked by Lance to "the OFFENDING" . . . and thus implicated with dangerous masculinity, but its contrasting story of thinking and planning ahead . . . is also characteristically linked to "grooming" which would be virtually impossible without precisely this kind of cleverness. Thus, a further dilemma for Lance in relation to dangerous masculinity may be that, as not all men's . . . behavior . . . is necessarily abusive, so all women's . . . thinking/planning, which may consider consequences, is, in the hands of men, not automatically nonabusive (pp. 127–128).

Through an understanding of such constructions, clinicians may help young men such as Lance to develop a nonabusive masculine identity and to become accountable for the choices that they make.

However, the authors treat their analysis of this case as the product of "interpretive repertoires" available to scholars in a given community at a particular point in time. Thus, they consider any text as open to re-analysis by those working in other theoretical frameworks or disciplines or at other points in time, arguing that any interpretation made is always, therefore, partial and underscoring the importance of explicit theory of the problem under study to their approach.

By relying on the close textual analytic approach of Gee (1991), the authors ground their analysis in the words and perspectives of the narrator. By incorporating within this approach the investigator's role in the interview and its analysis, the authors provide one way in which to integrate the context of narrative production into its analysis. By anchoring this context in a critical perspective on the problem under study, the authors show how theory of problem and method may be linked and how critical narrative analysis is well-suited for studies of individual cases involving lengthy transcriptions in which the analysts are also the interviewers.

Its primary limitation is the complexity posed by applying, in one approach, the number of analytic concepts employed in this approach. Indeed, Hiles and Cermák (2008) reduce critical narrative analysis to an analytic approach that emphasizes the "functionality" of an account or the type of account provided. They examine functionality in relation to the concept, positioning, examining the implications of how a narrator positions him or herself in a text.

CONTEXTUAL DISCURSIVE ANALYSIS

Corinne Squire wrote the volume, *HIV in South Africa: Talking About the Big Thing* (2007a). In this volume, Squire's intent was to bring a humanitarian crisis, the HIV epidemic in sub-Saharan Africa where rates of infection were close to 20% of 15- to 49-year-olds in 2007 (www.avert. irg/safricastats.htm), to the attention of the public and to explore how the victims of the crisis were living with and talking about HIV.

Working with a wide range of written documents gathered over a 5-year period of time, including government reports, magazine articles, and health education leaflets, as well as transcripts and notes from interviews with South Africans infected with or affected by HIV, she examined how individuals represented HIV to themselves and others, arguing that representation affects how one lives with HIV.

The examination involved a close analysis of the content and the structure of HIV narratives and the historical and political context for such speech. She calls her approach a *contextual discursive approach* to the texts that she studied. She concluded that her analysis showed: "people finding strategies to live with the condition in situations of medical underprovision, poverty, social discrimination and international neglect (p. 9)." Her work acts as a counterweight to "pathos and to paranoia" regarding the unfolding tragedy in South Africa, and it sheds light on how individuals might respond to other epidemics in the developing world.

Definition of Narrative

In this work, narrative is defined as a story, a story of a specific event or of a broad condition, which unfolds over time and with consequence within a specific social cultural milieu.

Theoretical Orientation

A *contextual discursive approach* to narrative requires a consideration of narrative in relation to the broad societal discourses to which it may be related, in relation to storytelling as a mode of communication, and in relation to the cultural representations to which it refers. Unlike a Foucauldian approach to discourse analysis, however, the approach requires a close analysis of the structure of narratives—that is, how people talk rather than how a historical social political context defines what is possible to say. Indeed, she referenced the work of Plummer (1995), who describes how individual storytelling—especially in relation to stigmatized identities—requires and also creates communities willing to listen.

Central Question

A primary question in this form of analysis is: How do individuals use and remake the representational forms on which they draw to tell the stories of their lives?

Major Concepts

The major concepts and assumptions of this approach reflect movements within narrative inquiry over the past 20 years. Thus, the analysis is approached in relation to the contexts in which narratives are told, co-constructed, performed, and lived.

HIV in South Africa: Talking About the Big Thing focuses on genre as the cultural form on which individuals rely to tell their stories. Squire's use of the term, *genre*, is compatible with that of other social scientists who treat it as a "convention of discourse" that relies on characters and plot. This contrasts with the use of the term within literature, where it has been employed in relation to a work's form (prose or poetry), mood (comedy or tragedy), or content (history or autobiography), for example (Chamberlain & Thompson, 1998). However, social scientists and literary scholars might agree that however defined, genres shape the meaning of stories told for both storytellers and their audiences, and they have the capacity to change over time (*see* Todorov [1990] for a discussion of genre in discourse).

In this volume, genres are discussed specifically as forms through which individuals counter externalization of a frightening phenomenon such as HIV for which there is no cure; undo stigma; educate; expand the community willing to listen; and claim citizenship. They are also presented as overlapping and fluid and as vehicles through which difficult emotions may be represented rather than merely expressed. This is particularly important in relation to a phenomenon such as HIV that promotes rejection by others.

Drawing on the work of Kristeva (1980/1982) and her concept of the *abject*, Squire examines narratives in relation to not only what research participants say but also what they cannot say and must represent symbolically.[1] She observes, for example:

> There were many occasions on which the socialized and sexualised abjection of HIV was described, and sometimes analysed, within the interviews. People told us about family members who "accepted" their status, yet did not touch them and refused the food they cooked . . . [w]omen interviewees . . . described feeling on the borders of religious community, "abject," between exclusion and inclusion, sometimes attending churches but not "saved", because their status as mothers outside marriage made this impossible in the evangelical congregations that constituted their faith communities (pp. 148–149).

Thus, the self that is negotiated within the HIV narratives is in negotiation with a "non-self" or "non-person of people's fears for its citizenly existence."

Squire asserts that genres operate as "local" theories to explain events that are misunderstood. Drawing on the work of West (1989), she considers these theories to be *pragmatic* in nature, aiming to provide a way to understand and to act in response to the pandemic rather than to provide "a permanent explanation" for both.

Orientation to Method

The approach depends on an immersion in the phenomenon under study (Squire conducted prior research on HIV in the U.K.); an ethnographic sensibility (she collected a wide range of documents and interview data over a 5-year period); and, informed by both, the development of a detailed description of the "global, local and historical realities" relevant to the research focus.

Interviews are transcribed verbatim. (In Squire's study, the transcriptions were also translated into English. Some but not all paralinguistic features were included in the translations because it was too difficult to identify their meaning from one language system to another.)

Transcriptions are examined to distinguish narrative from non-narrative material. A close reading of the narrative material is undertaken, attending to not only what is said but also how it is said in relation to the context in which it is spoken.

ILLUSTRATION

Along with the collection and examination of documents relevant to HIV, Squire conducted 37 interviews with HIV-infected or -affected research participants drawn from three townships around Cape Town. About half the interviews were conducted with individuals alone, the other half with individuals in small groups. The former strategy was considered ideal for self-disclosure, the latter for articulation of the range of issues raised by living with HIV. Some interviewees were interviewed a second and a third time. The relatively unstructured interviews covered topics such as types of support available to participants as well as their relationships and views of religion, community, and the government.

A close reading of the interview transcripts in relation to an understanding of the South African context yielded an identification of the prevailing genres on which victims of the HIV epidemic relied to represent their experiences: a "speaking out genre" (or an intimate disclosure story) in which individuals disclose and accept their HIV status; a "conversion genre" in which individuals move from believing that they will die from HIV to believing that they can live with HIV; and a "political genre" that resonates with South Africa's history of witnessing and resisting apartheid, as well as what was "unspeakable" about HIV within the South African context.

For example, intimate disclosure narratives tend to move from ignorance in relation to the condition to knowledge, acceptance, and then action; conversion narratives tend to frame acceptance as a spiritual task, to lift anxieties about HIV, and to refer to biblical passages in which God protects; the political narratives tend to position individuals as equivalent to other citizens and in relation to the experience of struggle against apartheid

An illustration of the conversion narrative is in Box 7–1 (Squire, 2007a, p. 159).

Box 7–1

Linda: Okay! In the first place I am glad that I know of my HIV positive status because now I know what to do. Then my husband, the one I am married to, I told him. At first, he could not accept it, he gave me too many problems. I then continued talking about it everyday... Truly, eventually he accepted it. It was before my baby was not discharged yet, so that/he could be tested as well./okay!/ Then he asked about the baby. I said the baby will be tested at nine months... Truly then I was told that the baby, I was very happy, because I was happy to save my baby. AZT helped me, my baby was tested negative ... so today I am not ready, I am not yet free, I don't feel like I am open. I am not open yet to stand up and say I have HIV. I will keep trying, you understand? /Mhm/ But I feel alright, most importantly I thank God. God said these things before, he said there will be these incurable diseases, so I believe in God truly. What he talked about, is happening today. So that is something else that inspired me, because God mentioned this before, he said they will happen, they are happening today, unto people, they would not in steep places, so I believe in that.

Source: Squire, C. (2007). *HIV in South Africa: Talking about the big thing*. London: Routledge.

Squire notes that this genre reproduces the moral force of religious conversion in the conversion from disbelief to acceptance of HIV. It anticipates the move of narrators into political action in the community, and it helps individuals to resist marginalization. Thus, it is more than "just talk": Conversion narratives may be understood as a social practice.

CONCLUSION

This chapter has highlighted two emerging approaches to narrative analysis: critical narrative analysis and discursive contextual analysis.

Critical narrative analysis has much in common with psycho-analysis in that the narrative analyst takes seemingly disconnected parts of an individual's story, generated through skillful and open-ended interviewing, and reassembles them into a new and coherent narrative. Unlike psychoanalysis, however, the individual completing the reconstruction is a narrative analyst (rather than the narrator), and there is great attention, in the final reports, to the narrator's (rather than the analyst's) words (*see* Chamberlain & Thompson's [1998] volume, *Narrative and Genre*, for a useful discussion of this issue.) Thus, critical narrative analysis is suited ideally to studies of clinical phenomena relying on a few research participants. The primary limitation of critical narrative analysis is the number of analytic concepts employed in this procedure.

Although perhaps not intended as a way to advance a new method of narrative analysis, a discursive contextual analysis of the sort developed in the volume *HIV in South Africa: Talking About the Big Thing* has significant potential for research on social work-related problems. By linking an individual's narrative to widely circulating genres within an individual's society, this approach could be used for study of many conditions that affect the individual's capacity to claim citizenship, broadly defined, within their communities; it resonates with social work's emphasis on understanding the person in the context of his or her environment; and it carries implications for psychosocial work with individuals, groups, and communities.

On the other hand, genres and cultural stories, in general, may reify culture or minimize the importance of individual stories, and "the political shapes of narratives . . . [may be] larger than a 'cultural' analysis can indicate (Squire, 2008, p. 57)." For example, in evaluating one of the stories her research participant tells as a conversion narrative, Squire wonders whether she is "erasing the particularity of her language and experience . . . (p. 57)."

Nonetheless, both the work of Emerson and Frosh and of Squire may be seen as part of a movement by scholars over the past 20 years to define genre; to understand life story, autobiography, and oral history in terms of genre; and to examine how genre (or "conventions of discourse" within a specific material and cultural context) and individual experience are inter-related (Chamberlain & Thompson, 1998).[2]

OVERVIEW AND CONCLUSION TO NARRATIVE ANALYTIC METHODS

What is gained or lost through the use of one approach to narrative analysis over another, however, may become part of a consideration of its trustworthiness. Moreover, whatever interpretation that is made does not have to rest on the claim that it is the only possible one; it need only rest on the claim that it is a viable one grounded in the assembled texts (Polkinghorne, 2007), a topic I take up in the final chapter of this volume.

8

Validation of Narrative Research

Some narrative reports do not address the issue of validity. This may reflect the field's preoccupation with discussion or demonstration of conceptual and methodological approaches to narrative analysis. Or, it may reflect doubts as to whether or not narrative inquiry could or should be considered scientific. Following Schiff (2006), I argue that narrative inquiry is scientific because it is based on observations, employs a set of concepts with which to understand what is observed, and strives to develop or illustrate theoretical concepts in ways that have significance beyond the initial observations. Therefore, narrative inquiry fulfills the basic requirements for science as it is understood in the natural sciences. The methods reviewed in this volume, for example, contain concepts necessary for the classification of phenomena observed and rules for explaining the patterns that emerge (Harré, 2004).

With that said, the question, Is a qualitative study valid?, is nonetheless a complex question to address, and it has been answered in varying ways (Mishler, 1990; Polkinghorne, 2007; Riessman, 2008; Seale, 2002; Shaw & Norton, 2008). In this chapter, I consider how validity has been framed in relation to qualitative research in general and narrative research in particular; I propose, drawing on the work of Hammersley (1992), a framework in which the *trustworthiness*, a broader concept than the validity, of narrative research may be considered; and I show how a consideration of reflexivity and ethics is crucial to assessments of the trustworthiness of any investigation.

APPROACHES TO VALIDITY

One's approach to validity depends ultimately on one's epistemological or political commitments (Riessman, 2008).[1] As a result, the validity question may be cast, for example, in terms of the truthfulness of what the narrator says, the meaningfulness of the investigator's interpretation of the narrator's story, or in relation to the power of the investigation considered as a whole to promote political change. Indeed, the validity question may even be dismissed as relatively unimportant because of the instability of social life (Guba & Lincoln, 1994) or dialogue (Silverman, 2004).

In this section, I emphasize validity in relation to investigators' interpretations of narratives; however, it is not the only way in which the question may be posed. My view is compatible with that of Runyan (1980), who, writing in relation to biography, asserts that any account of a life is inevitably affected by the personal, social, intellectual, and historical circumstances of its author; however, this acknowledgment does not preclude a rigorous evaluation of the quality of the evidence and logical inferences on which the account depends.

Scholars caution that interpretations should not be considered as valid or as invalid but, rather, as valid in varying degrees (Polkinghorne, 2007). Others suggest, considering validity in relation to research quality, that judgments of the quality of a study are never final and that they evolve in relation to the stage of research on the phenomenon under study (Shaw & Norton, 2008). In fact, Mishler (1990) argues that the concept *validity* should be replaced with the concept *validation*. In this view, a study would be considered to be validated, if investigators working in a relevant field come to rely on it for their own work; thus, the emphasis in Mishler's approach shifts responsibility for demonstration of validity from the individual investigator to a community of scholars.

However validity is conceptualized, the criteria used to assess validity cannot be used in a mechanical manner (Seale, 2002). Scholars must make judgments as to the extent to which a study conforms to accepted research practice (Mishler, 1990).[2]

FRAMEWORK FOR TRUSTWORTHINESS

Hammersley (1992) offers a useful framework with which one may consider the trustworthiness of narrative study that acknowledges the complexity and the communal nature of such assessments.[3] His framework depends on two presumptions: first, that scholars have confused *research-quality standards* with the *criteria used to assess such standards*; second, that criteria should be tailored to a specific research model. Thus, we should have differing assessment criteria for experimental and non-experimental research models and differing criteria for varying models of qualitative research within nonexperimental research.

The *standards* he advances (and believes should be applied to any type of social scientific research) are *truth* (i.e., validity) and *relevance* (i.e., use). With respect to validity, he argues that an account is valid if it represents the features of the phenomenon it is intended to describe, explain, or theorize. With respect to relevance, he argues that an account is relevant to a community of scholars if the study's topic is important and the study's findings make a significant contribution to knowledge.

The Validity Standard

In Hammersley's framework, assessment of validity hinges ultimately on the match between a study's evidence and central claims.

Criteria for Validity Assessment

Questions pertinent to validity assessment include such questions as these: Is the method appropriate for the study purpose? Is the method well-described? Have central aspects of the method been implemented? Is the study free of obvious error and bias? Have rival explanations been considered? These questions are, in effect, the criteria with which a study's validity is tested and echo those identified by Mishler (1990) in relation to assessing the validity of research that depends on narrative methods.

In short, the investigator uses the answers to these questions in order to form a judgment as to whether or not or the degree to which the study in question is valid. Thus, assessing validity is a complex task, requires consideration of all facets of the research enterprise and cannot be

---

Box 8–1

Questions to Guide Evaluation of the Validity of Narrative Studies

What were the conditions under which the narrative was produced, and what are the consequences of these conditions for interpretation of the narrative's meaning?

Has the full text subjected to analysis been included in the study report, or is it available to other scholars?

Have the analytic categories used in the analysis been specified, and is their relationship to the text (its structure and or content) clear?

Why do aspects of the text that do not support the major claims not undermine them?

Has the broad context in which the text was produced been discussed and its relevance for its interpretation examined?

---

reduced to a formulaic application of abstract principles or conformity to specific methodological practices.

Box 8–1 contains some questions scholars may pose in order to enhance the validity of their own narrative studies or to consider the validity of those conducted by others.

Information Required

To address such questions, studies need to be described so that the central conceptual and methodological issues raised by these questions can be evaluated. For example, investigators need to provide information as to how narrative is defined, the theoretical orientation out of which the study's method evolved, and its central orienting questions, major concepts, and methodological procedures, as illustrated in my discussion of exemplary narrative studies included in this volume. Additional information pertaining to the conditions of narrative production, analysis, and interpretation as articulated in the paragraphs below is also required.

Conditions of Narrative Production

In narrative research, it is important to specify the circumstances under which study data were obtained because the conditions of narrative production may suppress, encourage, or limit what the narrator says or contribute to gaps between what the narrator says and what the narrator means. For example, Mishler (1986a) discusses specific ways in which interviewers might affect research participants and speculates as to the significance of these circumstances for the narrative that is produced and its analysis. Polkinghorne (2007) specifies that validity assessments are aided by a discussion of the extent to which the interviewees feel safe in the interview, explore reflectively their experiences, handle aspects of experience that might be considered socially undesirable, and respond to the interviewer's person and conduct and/or talk in the interview.

Inclusion of Narrative Text

It is important to audio-record interviews to obtain the exact words of the interviewee and interviewer. It is not always obvious, however, how much of a verbatim transcription of the audio-recording to include in a study report. Some investigators make a transcribed text in its entirety available to the public. However, some research participants are reluctant to agree to this as a condition of their participation because full disclosure might compromise their anonymity. Others wish their names to be included in research reports, as they consider their narratives public testimonies to the need for social change (Squire, 2007a).

Irrespective of the amount of text displayed, it is important to describe where in the transcription the excerpted material falls and to include a summary of the material that preceded and follows the portion of the text that is displayed. In this way, the reader will be able to understand the context for the narrative and consider its implications for the adequacy of the analysis.

Analysis of Text

Narrative methods depend on careful attention to language. Pairing the verbatim text of a narrative with an analysis of its language is central to a reader's ability to evaluate the investigator's claims against the evidence at hand. Sometimes it is more powerful to provide a shorter but more fully analyzed text than a longer text with a less dense analysis (Silverman, 2004)—but not always. Other times, validity is enhanced when the investigator can identify and interpret where stories pull apart and together at the same time (Riessman, 2008).

Claims and Counter-claims

There is not agreement as to the utility of returning analyses of texts to narrators for comment. Some argue that it is useful to provide narrators the opportunity to clarify what they said and to confirm that the analysis conforms to their understanding of their experience (Polkinghorne, 2007). I caution that disavowals of interpretations do not necessarily mean that interpretations are lacking in validity.

Indeed, in my experience, narrators are sometimes surprised (and perhaps discouraged) to find, when presented with verbatim transcriptions of interviews with them, that they were less clear than they had assumed themselves to be. When presented with analyses of such interviews, some feel "objectified" as a result of the re-presentation of their spoken stories as written text. Short of engaging research participants as co-researchers, an approach linked to participatory action research (Reason & Bradbury, 2001), the utility of member checking might best be considered on a case-by-case basis.

The Relevance Standard

The relevance of research, the second standard against which social scientific research should be judged, is a function of the collective judgment of scholars over time (Hammersley, 1992). As a result, the relevance of findings cannot be asserted in advance of the completion of an investigation, and Hammersley argues that it cannot even be determined immediately after its conclusion.

Nonetheless, the relevance of a narrative study's contribution will emerge: It may depend on the method employed or on the problem under study; it may depend on a work's contribution to conceptually-anchored description, to clarification of a hypothesis or conceptualization of a process, or to elaboration or falsification of an existing theory; or it may depend on a work's relevance to professional practice. However, conceptualizing what constitutes adequate use is less straightforward because use may change over time.

Establishing relevance in all of these cases, however, may hinge on the investigator's ability to help the reader to understand the nonobvious meanings of the narratives studied and how an individual study fits within a larger body of work. Josselson (2006) sharpens the point for narrative studies when she asks whether each study should be considered an independent "finely wrought miniature" work of art or part of a "joint multilayered jigsaw puzzle, each one contributing a piece."

Elaborating my conviction that the latter metaphor is the one that is most apt, Josselson (2006) presents a thought-provoking analysis as to how narrative studies might be integrated without losing attention to language and context that is the hallmark of narrative methods.[4]

REFLEXIVITY

Reflexivity is central to an assessment of the extent to which a narrative study is trustworthy—that is, whether others can depend on the claims the investigator makes. *Reflexivity* generally refers to the ways in which an investigator's experience and commitments shape his or her engagement in each element of the research process (Willig, 2001), although broader definitions have been provided (Macbeth, 2001). Within the context of research by social work scholars on social work practice, reflexivity is central because it allows one to "defamiliarize" oneself with prevailing assumptions and routines in order to examine them anew (White, 2001).

In the positivist research tradition, the influence of the researcher on the investigation is considered a source of bias. In the constructivist tradition, it is assumed that the researcher inevitably shapes the investigation in which he or she is engaged because "the view from nowhere is forever out of human reach (Pels, 2000, p. 17)." Within the latter framework, the central question is not how to control for "investigator bias" but rather how the investigator can use knowledge of him- or herself to enhance understanding of the phenomenon under study.

Types of Reflexivity

Finlay (2002) identifies five types of reflexivity. These types include reflexivity as *introspection*; reflexivity as *intersubjective reflection*; reflexivity as *mutual collaboration*; reflexivity as *social critique*; and reflexivity as *discursive deconstruction*. Each comes with its own problems and possibilities, although what is most important in the end is how well the investigator shows how his or her experience, circumstances, and pre-suppositions affected the research (Finlay, 2002).

Reflexivity as introspection may be considered in relation to the investigator's position and perspective. For example, in one study the investigator examined how her behavior in the research setting mirrored that of a research participant leading to a deeper understanding of the phenomenon under study (Finlay, 1998).

Intersubjective reflection may be considered in relation to conscious or nonconscious aspects of the relationship between the investigator and the research participant. For example, in one study the investigator examined how his identification with and liking of a research participant affected the analysis (Hollway & Jefferson, 2000).

Reflexivity as mutual collaboration may be considered in relation to the examination by the investigator and research participant of the process of research. Much participatory action research in which investigators and research participants collaborate to study a phenomenon could be reframed in this manner.

Reflexivity as social critique may be considered in relation to the difference in power between an investigator and research participant. For example, in one study the investigators discussed how they omitted prejudicial representations of one ethnic group by the group that they studied and suggested the complexities such omissions raised for knowledge development (Marshall, Woollett, & Dosanjh, 1998).

Reflexivity as discursive deconstruction may be considered in relation to the ambiguous nature of words and language. Here, the interest is in how language is used by both the investigator and the research participant to persuade. A highly relevant form of reflexivity within the context of narrative research, its implementation might involve consideration of how alternative ways of analyzing the same narrative would highlight differing interpretations. Hiles and Cermák (2008) advocate this strategy in their model of narrative-oriented inquiry. (On this point, I note that it is worth reviewing Runyan's [1980] demonstration of how, taken together, multiple accounts of the life of Lincoln produced over time yield a more complex and credible account of his life than any one account alone.)

Drawing on these five types of reflexivity, the questions in Box 8–2 are the sort an individual investigator/interviewer might ask in order to examine reflexively his or her own work:

Box 8–2

Reflexivity: Some Questions to Ask

What position have I adopted vis-à-vis the interviewee and with what consequences for the collection, analysis, and interpretation of data?

How did the interviewee and I respond emotionally to each other and with what consequences for the collection, analysis, and interpretation of data?

To what extent and how were research participants empowered by participation in the research project and with what consequences for the collection, analysis, and interpretation of data?

How might my theoretical assumptions and methodological strategies have affected the collection, analysis, and interpretation of data?

What alternative interpretations to the ones I have drawn are possible in relation to the data obtained?

As useful as addressing such questions may be to the development of knowledge, it is often difficult to publish papers containing responses to them because of limits on space, uncertain standards regarding the presentation and evaluation of such material, and discomfort, in some quarters, with research accounts in which the investigator is highly visible. Specification of the *most important way* in which reflexivity, however it is defined, affects an investigation is one pragmatic way in which to begin to address the issue.

Representation of Results

Reflexivity also calls into question traditional forms of *representing the results of research* (Macbeth, 2001). For those concerned with the researcher's position in the world, vis-à-vis such categories as social class, race, occupational attainment, and gender, for example, representation has taken an autobiographical turn. For those concerned with the text produced by the researcher, representation has departed from traditional forms for social scientific writing, and investigators have experimented with how to represent themselves and research participants in the text (Lather & Smithies, 1997). Writing in the first-person and acknowledging the inevitably partial and unstable nature of interpretations is one straightforward way in which to represent one's findings.

These strategies also suggest, however, some of the challenges of working reflexively. These include, for example, the possibility that attention to the experience and circumstance of the investigator, ironically, may work to undermine attention to the phenomenon under study, obscure the partial nature of any set of findings, or result in a downward spiral of deconstruction of perspectives (Finlay, 2002). Pels (2000), in fact, is cautiously pessimistic regarding a scholar's capacity for self-examination. He argues that most, however, do a good job of examining the opposition by which he means the work of other scholars. He observes that "[f]rom this it follows that reflexivity can never be comprehensively executed by the individual knower, but remains a distributed process which must partly be left to the agonistic play of forces in the scientific and the general public marketplace (p. 17)."

ETHICAL ISSUES

A serious consideration of reflexivity and, in particular, how to represent the results of a narrative analysis engenders a serious consideration of a core ethical question in narrative inquiry: Who "owns" the story that is told (Estroff, 1995)? This question and others to which it is related are those with which ethnographers have grappled for years (Mattingly, 2005). Ethnographers have examined questions such as, Should the investigator share his or her interpretations with the research participant? and How should the investigator respond to the participant's reactions to the analysis? This latter issue is particularly complex because, at its heart, narrative analysis involves the re-representation of someone's story, a re-representation that runs the risk of an implicit pathologization of the storyteller (Squire, 2008), especially in relation to stories of personal trouble.

Other ethical questions of import pertain to procedural ethics (Guillemin & Gillam, 2004). Procedural ethics refers to issues of concern to research committees such as Institutional Review Boards (IRBs) within the United States. The work of these boards is guided by federal regulation (Title 45, Part 46, of the U.S. Code of Federal Regulations) and is framed in relation to the principles of respect for persons, beneficence, and justice. Respect hinges on protection from harm and voluntary participation in research; beneficence hinges on the minimization of harm and maximization of benefit; and justice hinges on equal treatment of persons as subjects (Denzin & Giardina, 2007).

There has been considerable criticism of the way in which proposals for qualitative and interpretive research have been reviewed by IRBs using these principles (American Association of University Professors, 2001; Padgett, 2008). These criticisms include the charge that the boards limit or micromanage interpretive work in the social sciences and the humanities; that they do not address the ethical issues that arise in the actual practice of such research; and that they function primarily to protect institutions over individuals.

For example, some of the questions that arise in narrative inquiry cannot be accommodated easily within standard IRB framework—questions such as How can the research participant consent to an interview in which the questions and therefore responses to them cannot entirely be predicted in advance by either the investigator or the research participant? and How can the anonymity of the research participant be maintained in studies in which the participant has narrated important life experiences? (Mattingly, 2005).

Moreover, research participants who agree to participate in narrative studies may do so because they want, by telling about an experience, to help others. Thus, they want neither anonymity nor the data they provide to be treated as confidential. They wish, by way of contrast, to testify publicly as to how they overcame a difficulty or met an injustice. (Testimony, however, raises complex issues. Gready [2008] provides a compelling example of the ways in which those who testified at the South African Truth and Reconciliation Commission lost control over their narratives, when their stories were retold by others in differing contexts. In some instances, narrators were disempowered by the retellings, thereby replicating the very condition the commission sought to redress.)

Because the answers to ethical questions such as the ones I raise here cannot be standardized, some scholars have argued for education to help investigators understand the complexity of ethical issues rather than education to help investigators to conform to abstract ethical rules (Schwandt, 2007), whereas others have argued for a "vulnerable" research ethics in which judgments depend on the specific study problem, population, and method (Mattingly, 2005).

In short, there is not a universal position from which one can evaluate research ethics because the determination of what is ethical involves a deliberate assessment as to how issues pertaining to consent, anonymity, confidentiality, ownership, and authorship, for example, are to be handled in a specific research project as it unfolds over time (Mattingly, 2005). Thus, the questions I have articulated in this section could be used by investigators to examine the ethical issues that are especially relevant to narrative investigations.

CONCLUSION

In sum, in this chapter I have outlined the utility of Hammersley's approach to validity, as he articulates this approach in relation to the concept, *trustworthiness*. I have indicated the questions that need to be asked and the information that needs to be provided in order for narrative investigators, as well as other scholars, to assess the trustworthiness of narrative studies. I have emphasized the importance of a reflexive and an ethical analysis of one's work to an assessment of its validity and ultimate use.

Ending this book where I began, it is appropriate perhaps to reference MacIntrye (2007). In his volume, *After Virtue*, he argued that understanding what is ethical requires understanding the set of traditions—hence the stories—of which one is apart; he also expressed a concern that the relationship between narrative and life has been devalued. This volume is dedicated, in part, to promoting a deeper understanding of this connection in the context of social work research and practice.

Appendix 1

Overview of Narrative Analytic Methods

Appendix 1 Overview of Narrative Analytic Methods

Analytic Focus	Source	Definitional Parameters	
		Central Question	Major Concepts
Narrative Content			
Holistic Content	(Lieblich, Tuval-Mashiach, & Zilber, 1998)	What is the core pattern in the life story?	Global impression, theme, early memory
Narrative Identity	(McAdams, 1993)	What identity is constructed in the life story?	Narrative tone, personal imagery, thematic lines, ideological settings, pivotal scenes, and conflicting protagonists
Shared Narrative	(Shay, 1994)	What is the meaning of a shared experience to a group?	Common themes, themes in relation to a common story, common story in relation to a fictional story

(Continued)

Appendix 1 Overview of Narrative Analytic Methods (*Cont'd*)

Analytic Focus	Source	Definitional Parameters	
		Central Question	*Major Concepts*
Narrative Structure			
Sequence of Clauses	(Labov, 1972)	How can a narrative be identified in the flow of talk?	Elements of a narrative, types of evaluation clauses
Poetic Structure	(Gee, 1991)	What is a defensible interpretation of a narrative?	Levels of textual structure
Surface-Deep Structure	(Gregg, 2006)	How is identity represented in discourse in relation to its structure and implicit plot?	Bi-polar contrasts in relation to self, others, and events; mediating terms; episodic-plot structure; and foundational contrast and mediating term
Narrative in Context			
Critical Narrative Analysis	(Emerson & Frosh, 2004)	How does this person, in this context, get to give the account he or she does?	Organization of narrative as speech, plot, subject, and focus
Contextual Discursive Analysis	(Squire, 2007a)	How do individuals use and remake the representational forms on which they draw in order to tell the stories of their lives?	Genre, audience, symbolic representation

Appendix 2

Guidelines for Narrative Research Proposals

A proposal for a narrative inquiry addresses the same broad questions as a proposal for any empirical investigation in the social sciences, questions such as: What is the topic of study? How will the research proceed? Why is it important? However, some of the information that should be included in a narrative research proposal differs from the information that should be included in a hypothesis-testing, experimental, or statistically based research proposal. As a result, the guidelines below are tailored to narrative research.

The guidelines are organized in relation to six basic elements: Background of the study; research focus and questions; plan of inquiry; approach to analysis; potential significance of findings; and a statement as to how reflexivity and human subject concerns will be addressed in the study. Although the elements are presented separately, they should connect logically and represent a coherent whole. For example, if one were to rely on Labov's (1972) definition of narrative, it would make sense to approach sampling, transcription, and analysis of narratives following his lead. However, if one were to accept his definition but to depart from his approach to analysis, a rationale as to why would be important to include in the research plan.

The guidelines will be most helpful to investigators if they have had prior experience with analysis of narrative material, understand the theoretical foundations of the narrative analytic strategy they hope to employ, and have had supervised research interviewing experiences (Josselson & Lieblich, 2003). An understanding of the major traditions of qualitative research is also useful so that the narrative project may be situated properly within the interpretive tradition of research.

The guidelines follow the proposal elements listed by Josselson and Lieblich (2003); they incorporate specific suggestions for narrative study advanced by Squire (2007b); and they encourage use of clearly defined terms, justifications as to why one strategy has been chosen over other plausible ones, and use of exemplars of narrative investigations to illustrate points one wants to make (Ragin, Nagel, & White, 2004). Readers are encouraged to consult Padgett's (2008) discussion on how to write a research proposal for elaboration of issues relevant to seeking external funding for qualitative investigations of all types.

PROPOSAL ELEMENTS

Background of the Study

The background to the study includes the broad topic on which the work is to focus; its significance to social work or other related disciplines; the personal sources of investment in the topic; the relevant theoretical background; the current empirical studies and related methodologies; and ways in which current knowledge needs to be clarified or expanded.

Because narrative studies focus on meaning in context, the investigator needs to read widely in order to locate relevant conceptual frameworks and empirical investigations. For example, if the study is concerned with maternal experience of child custody loss, the investigator may wish to examine literature pertaining to other facets of maternal experience, other kinds of loss, and contrast and compare maternal and paternal experiences of parenting writ large to place the investigation in an appropriate theoretical and empirical context.

The background is not merely a list of potential theoretical frameworks or completed investigations in an area, but it is an integrative statement of how the investigator evaluates current knowledge.

A central task in narrative research proposals is to maintain a balance between keeping the inquiry sufficiently open and, at the same time, limiting the conceptual scope of the investigation sufficiently: thus, "to straddle the line between a necessary openness to phenomena" that are not yet known and "theoretical sophistication" that "stands in the wings to illuminate" the analysis (Josselson & Lieblich, 2003).

Research Focus and Questions

The section concerned with the focus of the research should follow logically from the background section.

In narrative study, the focus may be broad, and it may be captured in a paragraph or in question form. It is helpful to restrict the focus with respect to an aspect of a broad phenomenon, a subgroup of interest, and a relevant context.

However, some flexibility with respect to focus is important, as the focus may shift slightly in relation to what the investigator learns in the course of the study.

The focus of research should also include a statement that the topic of concern will be explored with a narrative method, an elaboration of the features of narrative work, and a comparison and contrast between narrative and other qualitative methods so that the thrust of the work will become clear from the outset.

Plan of Inquiry

The plan of inquiry should discuss why the research focus or questions should be explored within a narrative framework and the specific definition of narrative and the specific narrative analytic approach to be employed.

The proposal would be strengthened with a consideration of why one approach to analysis of narratives has been chosen over another. On the other hand, the plan does not need to include a justification of interpretive research or a rationale as to why a quantitative, hypothesis-testing, or experimental investigation will not be conducted.

Other subsections of this section of the proposal include design, sampling plan, recruitment of research participants, collection of data, and recording of interviews.

Design.   The design section of the research proposal names the study design, relying on standard social science textbooks on the topic. The typical design for narrative research is the case study design. The design needs to be stated, its features explored, and its rewards emphasized.

Sampling plan.   The sampling section of the research proposal articulates the type and number of research participants—defined in relation to context—to be included in the study and why they are being studied in relation to the research focus. Even if the investigator believes the number of research participants to be included cannot be specified in advance, peer review committees often require specification of the minimum number of participants a study is to involve. In my experience, the minimum number depends in part on the institutional culture in which an investigator is operating, the extent to which its norms support qualitative research, and the persuasiveness with which the investigator articulates a scientific rationale for the study plan. As a result, some committees allow 1 participant, others require 5, and a few require at least 35. Josselson and Lieblich (2003) suggest a number between 5 and 30 participants.

It is useful to note the observation of Josselson and Lieblich (2003) on this point: "[T]he question of number of participants is one of the thorniest we have run into in committee meetings (p. 267)." They note that the received wisdom is that students should collect data until no new information is obtained or until they reach a point of "saturation," borrowing a concept from the constant comparative method. They note further, however, that "[n]either of us have ever reached any kind of saturation in our work—rather, we stop interviewing when we 'feel' saturated—that is we already have learned more than we will ever be able to contain and communicate (p. 267)." Thus, the concept of saturation may work "as a dodge" rather than as a useful concept with respect to specifying the number of participants to be included in a study.

Whether the project requires 1 research participant or 50, it is useful to remember that the relationship between the findings from an investigation of one group and their generalization to another group (or set of concepts) is highly problematic in all forms of research.

Recruitment of participants.   The plan should also state how participants will be located and approached; what they will be told regarding the study; how recruitment might affect the data; and by whom and under what conditions will research participants be interviewed, as well as how the study will conform to institutional requirements for the ethical conduct of research.

Moreover, attention should be paid to the ethical issues that may arise in narrative study such as how research participants will be alerted to the kinds of questions the investigator will ask, whether research participants will review transcripts or interpretations of the interviews with them, and how confidentiality will be maintained, if lengthy quotations are used in publications.

Data collection and recording.   The plan should include the qualitative interview format selected (Patton, 2002); if relevant, the specific narrative interview employed; and scholars' prior experience with the interview.

The proposal may also include a consideration of why one type of interview has been selected over another, and it may include information from scholars who have had experience with the interview format selected. Silverman (2004) argues that pursuit of "experience" is not an adequate justification of the use of an open-ended interview. Rationale for selection should be linked to features of the interview form and process vis-à-vis the aims of the study.

The proposal should also state who will conduct interviews and where, the interviewer's level of training and experience with qualitative interviewing, and whether supervision of interviewing will be part of the work of data collection.

Technological developments have made high-quality recording possible. It is useful for the investigator to identify in the research proposal the type of recording device to be used and how sound recordings of interviews will be stored, transformed into compact discs, transcribed into text, and stored as text files.

Approach to Analysis

Transcriptions.   The approach to analysis should include a description of the notational system to be used to transcribe audio-recordings and the connection between the notational system and data-analytic process.

The description should make clear as to the education the transcriber will receive with respect to relevant research ethics, how the transcriber will be trained to use the notational system for transcription, and how the quality of the transcriptions will be assessed.

Proofreading.   The proposal should consider who will proofread the transcriptions in relation to the audio-recordings and whether or not research participants will proofread the texts and how their comments will be incorporated into the study.

Data display.   The proposal should consider how transcriptions will be incorporated into the research report. There are a variety of ways in which transcriptions could be used and the decisions on this point include whether raw or transcribed/analyzed interviews will be included; whether entire transcriptions or extracts will be included; whether edited transcriptions or summaries of transcriptions will be included, for example. A justification for the method of data display chosen should be provided.

Data analysis.   The research proposal should identify and explain fully the type of narrative analytic procedure to be employed—for example, procedures to analyze content, structure, context, or the relationships among or beyond them pertaining to broader cultural discourses upon which they draw. As suggested in Chapter 3, data may include, in addition to transcribed texts, field notes pertaining to the performance of narratives, the audience for the narrative, or the local cultural or professional contexts in which the narratives might usefully be understood.

The inclusion of an exemplar of the data-analytic approach to be used in the study would enhance the credibility of the approach as well as specify the method.

Josselson and Lielich (2003) emphasize the utility for students and for their dissertation committees for the research proposal process to include a demonstration of the students' interviewing and data analytic skills. (For example, a student might bring a video of an interview and a preliminary narrative analysis of a portion of the interview transcribed into text.) They rightfully stress the importance of interviewing skills to the success of narrative study.

They note that we approve "the student for the work as much as the work itself (p. 272)" because narrative inquiry requires the ability to tolerate ambiguity, the intent to read widely, the capacity to interact skillfully with others as well as a "humanistic bent."

The proposal should address the role of research participants in the analytic process and toward what end.

Validity.   The research proposal should address the way in which the validity of the research will be conceptualized and measured. Following Hammersley (1992), for example, conceptualization of validity would hinge on the match between a study's evidence and central claims.

In a narrative proposal adopting this view, therefore, the proposal would include statements as to the fit between the narrative method and the research focus. It would further assert that the final study report would include excerpts from the transcribed text and illustrations as to how the text was analyzed, and it would evaluate the study in relation to the specific quality standards for the narrative analytic approach employed. Within narrative study, these standards may be implicit rather than explicit, and the investigator may have to turn to exemplars of the approach in order to conceptualize criteria with which to evaluate closely his or her work.

Potential Significance of Findings

The research proposal should address the potential significance of the narrative study. This section may be in the first section of the proposal that considers the background to the proposed study or it may be treated separately and presented after a consideration of the validity of study findings.

Again following Hammersley (1992), the significance of findings cannot be specified fully in advance of the completion of an empirical investigation and, indeed, at its conclusion. However, it is possible to clarify the expected or hoped for contribution. Narrative work may contribute, for example, to description that relies on social scientific concepts (rather than exclusively those of research participants), to clarification of a process, or to elaboration of an existing theory. If the latter is the aim of the study, it is important that potential significance be framed in terms of theoretical rather than empirical generalization.

Careful qualification of findings is crucial in empirical research of all kinds. In narrative work, it is important to specify the circumstances under which the data were obtained, to discuss issues pertaining to reflexivity noted below, and to consider both in relation to their potential significance for the study findings.

It is also important not to make erroneous assumptions regarding the stability of an individual's social context or the relationship between an individual's narrative and actions (Silverman, 2004). However, a caution against inadequate qualification or inappropriate generalization does not rule out creative speculation as to the significance of a work.

Ultimately, the significance of a narrative inquiry depends on the investigator's ability to help the reader to understand the nonobvious meanings of the narratives studied as well as their larger significance. Indeed, much interesting work in narrative illustrates a conceptual approach to a problem or implementation of a method.

Consideration of Reflexivity, Human Subject, and Ethical Concerns

The plan should include a section devoted to how the investigator's characteristics or experiences might affect the proposed research—the way in which the research question or focus is framed, the way in which the interviewees respond to the questions asked, the way in which the data analysis may be shaped, for example. Josselson and Lieblich emphasize Van Manen's point (1990) that orientation to an investigation involves adopting a vantage point and, in one sense, reflexivity.

Information pertaining to reflexivity may be distributed throughout the research proposal, or it may be placed at the end of the proposal. What sort of information and how much information to include, however, is not obvious. From my view, brief concise statements directed at specific issues relevant to the conceptualization or implementation of the research is most helpful to readers of the work.

In addition to traditional ethical issues that must be addressed to fulfill requirements of research committees such as Institutional Review Boards in the United States, attention should also be paid to the ethical issues that may arise in narrative study such as how research participants will be alerted to the kinds of questions the investigator will ask, whether research participants will review transcripts or interpretations of the interviews with them, and how confidentiality will be maintained, if lengthy quotations are used in publications.

Notes

CHAPTER 1

1.1 Indeed, narrative inquiry is expanding in multiple directions. For example, a recent call for papers from the International Society for Cultural History and Cultural Studies, with the support of the National Human Rights Commission of Mexico, illustrates how narrative studies traverse the boundary between the humanities and the social sciences (and, by implication, the professions) and between one language group and another, engage in topics such as "text, context and intertext in storytelling and performance," "children's stories—language, authority, and silence," "memory and truth telling," and "globalization and indigenous cultures," and connect to social justice concerns (http://enkidumagazine.com/chic.esc.htm).

CHAPTER 2

2.1 The work of Hollway and Jefferson (2000) into the effects of anxiety on fear of crime is one exception. In this study, the research design (the case study), the method of data collection (open-ended "free association" narrative interviews), and the approach to data analysis are explicitly linked to psychodynamic assumptions about the self and subjectivity. There is a theoretical coherence to their work.

2.2 In analytic induction, the investigator begins a study with a hypothesis drawn from the literature, examines the fit between the hypothesis and the study data, and alters the hypothesis as necessary until the investigator can account theoretically for the data obtained. Typically, this process proceeds as follows: the original hypothesis is tested against interview data from the first research participant and revised as necessary so that the hypothesis fits the data; the revised hypothesis is then tested against interview data from the second research participant and revised as necessary and so on, until all the relevant data from all research participants have been tested and a final revised hypothesis posed.

> Most narrative investigations produce explanations, and, as a result, the *logic of analytic induction*—the attempt to develop explanations through careful test of ideas against data—is appropriate for this sort of work. However, the *method of analytic induction*, testing specific hypotheses against evidence, is less so because narrative investigations develop complex and interlocking interpretations of storied data rather than single hypotheses, and they depend on detailed approaches to analysis. Indeed, some scholars argue against reduction of complex case studies to a few variables (Flyvberg, 2007).

2.3 Gobo (2007) shows the theoretical and practical problems associated with applying probability sampling to social research of all kinds and discusses why the social sciences must embrace and build on the strengths of nonprobability sampling. He highlights, in particular, the theoretical problems associated with a reliance on socio-economic variables to construct representative samples in studies of social-psychological phenomena whose distribution in a population is unknown.

2.4 Moreover, a strong defense of biographical work in the context of policy analysis and cross-cultural study has emerged in the United Kingdom (Chamberlayne, Bornat, & Wengrarf, 2000; Rustin & Chamberlayne, 2002). Such work allows investigators to "focus on the mystery which lies at the heart of social inquiry, the mutual shaping of individual lives and social structures" (Chamberlayne & King, 2000, p. 2), thereby underscoring C. Wright Mills' assertion that "no social study that does not come back to the problems of biography, of history and of their intersections within a society has completed its intellectual journey" (Mills, 2000, p. 6).

CHAPTER 3

3.1 Gubrium and Holstein (2009) consider *intertextuality* in relation to the work of Kristeva (1980), noting that the meaning of narratives is not transmitted directly from writer to reader but rather is "mediated by meanings of codes suggested to the writer and the reader by other texts. . . . [and] that any episode of storytelling should be viewed as sharing the empirical stage with other stories (pp. 186–187)." These influences are neither conscious nor intentional but rather reflect the broad cultural milieu of which a text is a part.

3.2 In my own work, I have used Olympus digital voice recorders to record interviews with research participants. I store the interviews as audio files in the recorder's folders. I then transfer the audio files from the recorder to my computer using a USB port, where they are stored as audio files in the "My Documents" section of my computer. I then download the audio files from my computer to a compact disk. After making a copy of the disk for my records, I send one disk to a transcriber. The transcriber uploads the audio files from the compact disk onto his or her computer. To transcribe the audio files, some transcribers use the Olympus transcription kit. The kit contains a software program that enables the audio file to be played and a foot-pedal that allows the transcriber to move back and forth on the file so that the transcriber's hands are free to type what he or she hears. Advances in the technology of recording or videotaping will not eliminate the judgments that have to be made in order to transform oral speech into written text (Mishler, 1991).

CHAPTER 4

4.1 Brown and her colleagues were interested in understanding how individuals construct moral problems in relation to two concepts: justice and care. They developed a guide, rather than a "coding manual," for investigators to use with complex narratives elicited by questions such as: Please tell about a situation in which you did not know what was the right thing to do. Operating from a specific theoretical framework in relation to moral judgment, the guide provides readers with a way to understand the research participant's moral conflict or "voice" and how the participant frames him or her self in relation to the conflict and the choices the research participant made.

4.2 Mishler (1995) proposed a typology of narrative analysis based on Halliday's (1973) three-part classification of the function of language: models that focus on representation (the correspondence between the sequence of events in life and in story), models that focus on the structure of language (how narratives are constructed), and models that focus on the function of language (the purposes and effects of stories). He identifies Shay's (1994) volume, *Achilles in Vietnam*, as falling into one category of the first type that attempts to "reconstruct the told from the telling." In this method, investigators collect a large number of stories. Typically, however, the stories are not told in chronological order. The investigator reassembles each story in chronological order and then identifies a narrative or story that is common to each one.

CHAPTER 5

5.1 In his later work, Labov (1997) emphasized that narratives inevitably contain a theory of causality of the "most reportable event" in the story; that this theory, in turn, assigns praise and blame; and, as such, that narratives are told from the point of view of the narrator within an implicit ideological framework.

5.2 To understand Gregg's use of Lévi-Strauss and of Propp, it is helpful to summarize the relevant concepts of each. The work of Lévi-Strauss is concerned with traditional narratives or myths. His basic claim is that all myths deal with a limited number of themes (Johnstone, 2001). Specifically, he argues that although myths vary in manifest content, they often share a deep structure (that is, a fundamental binary opposition such as nature vs. culture). He considers these oppositions to be unconscious and inherent to human mental processes. The tension created by a binary opposition is mediated by a third idea or solution. In this way, a myth becomes a tool through which inherent contradictions within societies are addressed. Gregg adopts Lévi-Strauss' ideas of *surface structure, deep structure, binary opposition*, and *mediation*, but he applies them to a study of identity rather than to a study of traditional narrative.

Propp's (1928/1968) interest is folktales. His basic claim is that the folktales he studied contain the same structure or sequence of meaningful actions by characters (Johnstone, 2001). Specifically, through an analysis of the components of Slavic fairytales, Propp identified 31 units, including elements that *introduce the situation* (such as *interdiction* in which a hero is warned); that *contain the body of the story* (such as *a lack* in which a need is indentified); that *articulate the donor sequence* in which the hero searches for a method to resolve the lack (such as *testing* in which the hero is challenged to prove heroic qualities); and that *describe the hero's return* (such as transfiguration in which the hero is given a new appearance). Not all stories contain all elements, but they typically occur in the order noted above.

Gregg adopts Propp's idea of an invariant sequence of events, but he applies them to a study of identity rather than to a study of a set of folktales.

CHAPTER 6

6.1 The handbook edited by Schiffrin, Tannen, and Hamilton (2001) and the one by van Dijk (1985) provide information on a range of approaches to discourse analysis.

6.2 Critical discourse analysis (CDA) has been described as the "intellectual cousin" (Seale, Gubo, Gubrium, & Silverman, 2007) of discourse analysis. It is best described as a school of varying perspectives and methods all of which are concerned with understanding how social control is expressed in language (Wodak, 2007). Its primary aim is to show how language oppresses and how it may be used to enlighten or empower. CDA embraces a problem-oriented approach to research; examines the context of the problem under study through fieldwork and analysis of the historical contexts in which the problem is embedded; and is methodologically eclectic; however, sociolinguistic analysis remains a key feature of the approach. There are two widely recognized approaches to CDA: that of Fairclough (1992) and that of Wodak (Wodak, 2001). It is similar in spirit to FDA. For example, in Fairclough's approach, three levels of discourse are examined—written and spoken texts; processes of text production, distribution, and consumption; and social practices that shape discourse as ideology. One exemplar of this method is that of Woodside-Jiron (2004), who examined how radical changes in educational policy between 1995 and 1997 occurred in the State of California. She studied the language of relevant texts such as legislation, policy reports, and government documents; she traced political and policy changes during the time period under study; and she evaluated how reciprocal influences among texts and social practices made a redefinition of educational policy possible.

CHAPTER 7

7.1 Squire (2007a) elaborates Kristeva's concept, the abject, as follows:

A territory of disgust and horror, but also of fascination and even pleasure, the abject is for Kristeva an unavoidable part of subjects' relationship to language. It is produced at the moment when the subject separates itself from its infantile physical existence and enters the social world, and thus it has a particular relation to maternity, the body and its products . . . and to death, animality and 'others' who are not social subjects . . . It is on the border between subject and object, desire and thought, death and life (p. 148).

7.2 Roberts (2002) highlights the work of Ruth Finnegan (1998) as one exemplar of how to understand personal narratives in relation to widely circulating stories about social life. In her volume, *Tales of the City: A Study of Narrative and Urban Life*, she shows the interconnections of various myths of tales of the city.

CHAPTER 8

8.1 Participatory action research, as Riessman (2008) notes, repositions the validity question so that the community from which co-research participants come becomes part of the community that judges the trustworthiness of research they produce, thereby raising complex questions regarding for whom the co-research participants speak and on what grounds.

8.2 Moreover, what is considered as accepted research practice inevitably depends on the research model. As Polkinghorne (2007) observes:

[I]n the actual performance of validity judgments, the background beliefs and assumptions of different communities affect what they accept as legitimating evidence and sound reasoning. For example, a community that believes that only directly observable facts are adequate to support the validity of a claim would hold that no claim about people's mental lives could be justified or valid (p. 475).

8.3 Hammersley's (1992) approach to trustworthiness differs somewhat from the one advocated by Lincoln and Guba (1985). Hammersley uses the term, *trustworthiness*, to encompass two broad concepts, truth (or validity) and relevance, whereas Lincoln and Guba use the term to focus on one concept, validity. Hammersely considers validity in relation to the strength of inferences that may be drawn from any social scientific investigation, whereas Lincoln and Guba argue that validity must be tailored to special features of qualitative as compared to quantitative research. Moreover, Lincoln and Guba posit specific methodological strategies that they believe will enhance the validity of any qualitative investigation and these include strategies to increase the credibility, transferability, dependability, and confirmability of the research. A logical extension of their view is that these strategies constitute criteria against which all qualitative research, irrespective of method, should be judged. Hammersley argues that Lincoln and Guba, therefore, conflate research standards and the criteria used to assess them.

8.4 Efforts to integrate research also bring to the fore the importance of social work and other scholars working to create the conditions for communication with communities concerned with the problems they study. As West (1989) observes:

> [O]nce one gives up on the search for foundations and the quest for certainty [as is surely the case for scholars working with questions of the meaning of experience], human inquiry into truth and knowledge shifts to the social and communal circumstances under which persons can communicate and cooperate in the process of acquiring knowledge. What was once purely epistemological now highlights the values and operations of power requisite for the human production of truth and knowledge (p. 213).

References

Adler, A. (1931). *What life should mean to you.* Boston: Little Brown.

Adler, J., Kissel, E., & McAdams, D. (2006). Emerging from the CAVE: Attributional style and the narrative study of identity in midlife adults. *Cognitive Therapy and Research, 30*(1), 39–51.

American Association of University Professors (AAUP) (2001). Regulations governing research on human subjects: Academic freedom and the Institutional Review Board. *Academe, 67*(4), 358–370.

Anderson, E. (1999). *Code of the street.* New York: Norton.

Andrews, M., Squire, C., & Tamboukou, M. (Eds.). (2008). *Doing narrative research.* Los Angeles: Sage.

Antaki, C., Billig, M., Edwards, D., & Potter, J. (2003). Discourse analysis means doing analysis: A critique of six analytical shortcomings. *Discourse Analysis Online.* Retrieved March 5, 2010, from http://www.shu.ac.uk/daol/previous/v1/n1/index.htm.

Arribas-Ayllon, M. & Walkerdine, V. (2008). Foucauldian discourse analysis. In C. Willig & W. Stainton-Rogers (Eds.), *The Sage handbook of qualitative research in psychology* (pp. 91–108). London: Sage.

Atkinson, J. & Heritage, J. (1984). Transcript notation. In J. Atkinson & J. Heritage (Eds.), *Structures of social action: Studies in conversation analysis* (pp. ix–xvi). Cambridge: Cambridge University Press.

Atkinson, P. & Delamont, S. (2006). Rescuing narrative from qualitative research. *Narrative Inquiry, 16*(1), 164–172.

Bakhtin, M. (1981). *The dialogic imagination.* Austin: University of Texas Press.

Bakhtin, M. (1984). *Problems of Dostoevsky's poetics.* Minneapolis: University of Minnesota Press.

Bamberg, M. & Andrews, M. (Eds.). (2004). *Considering counter-narratives.* Amsterdam: John Benjamins.

Bar-On, D. (1991). Trying to understand what one is afraid to learn about. In D. Schon (Ed.), *The reflective turn: Case studies in and on educational practice* (pp. 321–342). New York: Teachers College, Columbia University.

Bar-On, D. (2006). *Tell your own story.* New York: CEU Press.

Bell, S. (2006). Intensive mothering in spite of it all. In A. De Fina, D. Schiffrin, & M. Bamberg (Eds.), *Discourse and identity* (pp. 233–251). Cambridge: Cambridge University Press.

Brown, L., Argyris, D., Attanucci, J., Bardige, B., Gilligan, C., Johnston, K., et al. (1988). *A guide to reading narratives of conflict and choice for self and voice.* Cambridge: Harvard University Press.

Bruner, J. (1990). *Acts of meaning.* Cambridge: Harvard University Press.

Bruner, J. (2004). The narrative creation of self. In L. Angus & J. & McLeod (Eds.), *The handbook of narrative and psychotherapy: Practice, theory, and research* (pp. 3–14). Thousand Oaks, CA: Sage.

Cain, C. (1991). Personal stories: Identity acquisition and self-understanding in Alcoholics Anonymous. *Ethos, 19*(2), 210–253.

Campbell, D. (1975). "Degrees of freedom" and the case study. *Comparative Political Studies, 8*(2), 178–192.

Capps, L. & Ochs, E. (1995). *Constructing panic. The discourse of agoraphobia.* Cambridge: Harvard University Press.

Chamberlain, M. & Thompson, P. (1998). Genre and narrative in life stories. In M. Chamberlain & P. Thompson (Eds.), *Narrative and genre* (pp. 1–22). London: Routledge.

Chamberlayne, P., Bornat, J., & Wengraf, T. (2000). Introduction: The biographical turn. In P. Chamberlayne, J. Bornat, & T. Wengraf (Eds.), *The turn to biographical methods in social science: Comparative issues and examples* (pp. 1–30). London: Routledge.

Chamberlayne, P. & King, A. (2000). *Cultures of care: Biographies of careers in Britain and the two Germanies.* Bristol, UK: The Polity Press.

Charon, R. (2006). *Narrative medicine: Honoring the stories of illness.* Oxford: Oxford University Press.

Clandinin, D. (Ed.). (2007). *Handbook of narrative inquiry: Mapping a methodology.* Thousand Oaks, CA: Sage.

Clandinin, D. & Connelly, F. (2000). *Narrative inquiry: Experience and story in qualitative research.* San Francisco: Jossey-Bass.

Clavarino, A., Najman, J., & Silverman, D. (1995). The quality of qualitative data: Two strategies for analyzing medical interviews. *Qualitative Inquiry, 1*(2), 223–242.

Cooper, H. (2009). *Research synthesis and meta-analysis: A step-by-step approach* (4th ed.). Thousand Oaks, CA: Sage.

Cortazzi, M. (2001). Narrative analysis in ethnography. In P. Atkinson, A. Coffey, S. Delamont, J. Lofland, & L. Lofland (Eds.), *Handbook of ethnography* (pp. 384–394). Thousand Oaks, CA: Sage.

Coyle, A. (1995). Discourse analysis. In G. Breakwells, S. Hammond, & C. Fife-Schaw (Eds.), *Research methods in psychology* (pp. 243–258). London: Sage.

Crepeau, E. (2000). Reconstructing Gloria: A narrative analysis of team meetings. *Qualitative Health Research, 10*(6), 766–787.

Cronbach, L. (1975). Beyond the two disciplines of scientific psychology. *American Psychologist, 30*(2), 116–127.

Czarniawska, B. (2004). *Narratives in social science research.* London: Sage.

Davies, B. & Harré, R. (1990). Positioning: The discursive construction of selves. *Journal for the Theory of Social Behavior, 20,* 43–63.

Davies, B. & Harré, R. (1999). Positioning and personhood. In R. Harré & L. Van Langenhove (Eds.), *Positioning theory: Moral contexts of intentional action* (pp. 32–53). Malden, MA: Oxford.

De Fina, A., Schiffrin, D., & Bamberg, M. (2006a). Editors' Introduction to Part IV: The in-between self: Negotiating between person and place. In A. De Fina, D. Schiffrin, & M. Bamberg (Eds.), *Discourse and identity* (pp. 345–350). Cambridge: Cambridge University Press.

De Fina, A., Schiffrin, D., & Bamberg, M. (2006b). Editors' Introduction. In A. De Fina, D. Schiffrin, & M. Bamberg (Eds.), *Discourse and Identity* (pp. 1–23). Cambridge: Cambridge University Press.

Delgado, R. (1988). Storytelling for oppositionists and others: A plea for narrative. *Michigan Law Review, 87*(8), 2411–2441.

Dentith, S. (1995). *Bakhtinian thought: An introductory reader.* New York: Routledge.

Denzin, N. & Giardina, M. (2007). Introduction: Ethical futures in qualitative research. In N. Denzin & M. Giardina (Eds.), *Ethical futures in qualitative research: Decolonizing the politics of knowledge* (pp. 9–44). Walnut Creek, CA: Left Coast Press.

Doestoevsky, F. (1989). *Crime and punishment* (J. Coulson, Trans./G. Gibian, Ed.). (3rd. ed). NY: W. W. Norton. (Original work published 1866)

Edley, R. (2001). Analysing masculinity: Interpretative repertoires, ideological dilemmas and subject positions. In M. Wetherell, S. Taylor, & S. Yates (Eds.),

Discourse as data: A guide for analysis (pp. 189–228). London: The Open University.

Edvardsson, D., Rasmussen, B. H., & Riessman, C. (2003). Ward atmospheres of horror and healing: A comparative analysis of narrative. *Health: An Interdisciplinary Journal for the Social Study of Health, Illness, and Medicine, 7*(4), 377–396.

Elliott, J. (2005). *Using narrative in social research: Qualitative and quantitative approaches.* London: Sage.

Emerson, P. & Frosh, S. (2004). *Critical narrative analysis in psychology.* New York: Palgrave Macmillan.

Emerson, R., Fretz, R., & Shaw, L. (1995). *Writing ethnographic fieldnotes.* Chicago: University of Chicago Press.

Erikson, E. (1968). *Identity, youth, and crisis.* New York: Norton.

Estroff, S. (1995). Whose story is it anyway? In K. Combs, D. Bernard, & R. Carson (Eds.), *Chronic illness: From experience to policy* (pp. 77–192). Bloomington: Indiana University Press.

Fairclough, N. (1992). *Discourse and social change.* Cambridge: The Polity Press.

Fink, A. (2009). *Conducting research literature reviews* (3rd ed.). Thousand Oaks, CA: Sage.

Finlay, L. (1998). Reflexivity: An essential component for all research? *British Journal of Occupational Therapy, 61,* 453–456.

Finlay, L. (2002). Negotiating the swamp: The opportunity and challenge of reflexivity in research practice. *Qualitative Research, 2*(2), 209–230.

Finnegan, R. (1998). *Tales of the city: A study of narrative and urban life.* Cambridge: Cambridge University Press.

Flyvberg, B. (2007). Five misunderstandings about case-study research. In C. Seale, G. Gobo, J. Gubrium, & D. Silverman (Eds.), *Qualitative research practice* (pp. 390–404). London: Sage.

Fontana, A. & Prokos, A. (2007). *The interview: From formal to post-modern.* Walnut Creek, CA: Left Coast Press.

Freeman, M. (2007). Narrative and relation: The place of the other in the story of the self. In R. Josselson, A. Lieblich, & D. McAdams (Eds.), *The meaning of others: Narrative studies of relationships* (pp. 11–20). Washington, DC: American Psychological Association.

Frosh, S. (2002). *After words: The personal in gender, culture and psychotherapy.* New York: Palgrave.

Frosh, S. (2003). Psychosocial studies and psychology: Is a critical approach emerging? *Human Relations, 56*(12), 1545–1567.

Frosh, S. (2007). Disintegrating qualitative research. *Theory and Psychology Online, 17,* 635–653.

Frosh, S. & Saville Young, L. (in press). The psychoanalytic psychosocial. In J. Mason & A. Dale (Eds.), *Social researching: New perspectives in methods.* London: Sage.

Gee, J. P. (1985). The narrativization of experience in the oral style. *Journal of Education, 167*(11), 9–35.

Gee, J. P. (1991). A linguistic approach to narrative. *Journal of Narrative and Life History, 1*(1), 15–39.

Gee, J. P. (1996). *Social linguistics and literacies: Ideology in discourses.* London: Falmer.

Gee, J. P. (2005). *An introduction to discourse analysis: Theory and method* (2nd ed.). London: Routledge.

Georgakopoulou, A. (2006). The other side of the story. Towards a narrative analysis of narratives-in-interaction. *Discourse Studies, 8*(2), 235–257.

Gergen, K. (2009). *An invitation to social construction* (2nd ed.). Los Angeles: Sage.

Gilgun, J. (1994). A case for case studies in social work research. *Social Work, 39*(4), 371–380.

Gilgun, J. (1995). We shared something special: The moral discourse of incest perpetrators. *Journal of Marriage and the Family, 57*(2), 265–281.

Gillies, V. (1999). An analysis of the discursive positions of women smokers: Implications for practical intervention. In C. Willig (Ed.), *Applied discourse analysis* (pp. 66–86). Buckingham, UK: Open University Press.

Glaser, B. & Strauss, A. (1967). *The discovery of grounded theory.* Chicago: Aldine.

Gobo, G. (2007). Sampling, representativeness and generalizability. In C. Seale, G. Gobo, J. Gubrium, & D. Silverman (Eds.), *Qualitative research practice* (pp. 405–426). London: Sage.

Goffman, E. (1959). *The presentation of self in everyday life.* Garden City, NJ: Doubleday.

Gready, P. (2008). The public life of narratives: Ethics, politics, and methods. In M. Andrews, C. Squire, & M. Tamboukou (Eds.), *Doing narrative research* (pp. 137–150). Los Angeles: Sage.

Gregg, G. S. (2006). The raw and the bland: A structural model of narrative identity. In D. McAdams, R. Josselson, & A. Lieblich (Eds.), *Identity and story: Creating self in narrative* (pp. 63–87). Washington, DC: American Psychological Association.

Greimas, A. & Courtés, J. (1982). *Semiotics and language: An analytical dictionary* (L. Crist, Trans.). Bloomington: Indiana University Press.

Guba, E. & Lincoln, Y. (1994). Competing paradigms in qualitative research. In N. Denzin & Y. Lincoln (Eds.), *Handbook of qualitative research* (pp. 105–117). Thousand Oaks, CA: Sage.

Gubrium, J. & Holstein, J. (2009). *Analyzing narrative reality*. Los Angeles: Sage.

Guillemin, M. & Gillam, L. (2004). Ethics, reflexivity, and "ethically important moments" in research. *Qualitative Inquiry, 10*(2), 261–280.

Gulich, E. & Quasthoff, U. (1985). Narrative analysis. In T. van Dijk (Ed.), *Handbook of discourse analysis* (pp. 169–198). London: Academic Press.

Hall, C. (1997). *Social work as narrative: Storytelling and persuasion in professional texts*. Aldershot, UK: Ashgate.

Hall, C., Jokinen, A., & Suoninen, E. (2003). Legitimating the rejecting of your child in a social work meeting. In C. Hall (Ed.), Constructing clienthood in social work and human services: Interaction, identities, and practices (pp. 27–43). London: Jessica Kinglsey.

Hall, C., Slembrouck, S., & Sarangi, S. (2006). *Language practices in social work*. London: Routledge.

Hall, C. & Slembrouck, S. (in press). Interviewing parents of children in care: Perspectives, discourses, and accountability. *Children and Youth Services Review*.

Hammersley, M. (1992). *What's wrong with ethnography?* London: Routledge.

Hardy, T. (1891/2008). *Tess of the d'Urbervilles*. Oxford: Oxford University Press.

Harré, R. (2004). Staking our claim for qualitative research as a science. *Qualitative Research in Psychology, 1*, 3–14.

Harré, R. & van Langenhove, L. (Eds.) (1999). *Positioning theory: Moral contexts of intentional action*. Oxford: Blackwell Publishers.

Hepburn, A. & Potter, J. (2007). Discourse analytic practice. In C. Seale, G. Gobo, J. Gubrium, & D. Silverman (Eds.), *Qualitative research practice* (pp. 168–184). London: Sage.

Herman, L. & Vervaeck, B. (2001). *Handbook of narrative analysis*. Lincoln: University of Nebraska Press.

Hiles, D. & Cermák, I. (2008). Narrative psychology. In C. Willig & W. Stainton-Rogers (Eds.), *The Sage Handbook of qualitative research in psychology* (pp. 147–164). London: Sage.

Hinchman, L. & Hinchman, S. (1997). Introduction. In L. Hinchman & S. Hinchman (Eds.), *Memory, identity, community: The idea of narrative in the human sciences* (pp. xiii–xxxii). Albany: State University of New York Press.

Hollway, W. & Jefferson, T. (2000). *Doing qualitative research differently: free association, narrative, and the interview method*. London: Sage.

Holstein, J. (1988). Studying family usage: Family image and discourse in mental hospitalization decisions. *Journal of Contemporary Ethnography, 17*, 262–284.

Homer. (1974). *Iliad* (R. Fitzgerald, Trans.). New York: Anchor-Doubleday. (Original not dated)

Hydén, M. (1995). Verbal aggression as prehistory of woman battering. *Journal of Family Violence, 10*(1), 55–71.

Hydén, M. (2008). Narrating sensitive topics. In M. Andrews, C. Squire, & M. Tamboukou (Eds.), *Doing narrative research* (pp. 121–136). Los Angeles: Sage.

Hydén, M. & Överlien, C. (2004). "Doing" narrative analysis. In D. Padgett (Ed.), *The qualitative research experience* (pp. 250–268). Belmont, CA: Thomson Brooks/Cole.

Jefferson, G. (2004). Glossary of transcript symbols with an introduction. In G. Lerner (Ed.), *Conversation analysis: Studies from the first generation* (pp. 13–31). Amsterdam: John Benjamins.

Johnstone, B. (2001). Discourse analysis and narrative. In D. Schiffrin, D. Tannen, & H. Hamilton (Eds.), *The handbook of discourse analysis* (pp. 635–649). Malden, MA: Blackwell.

Josselson, R. (2006). Narrative research and the challenge of accumulating knowledge. *Narrative Inquiry, 16*(1), 3–10.

Josselson, R. & Lieblich, A. (2002). A framework for narrative research proposals in psychology. In R. Josselson, A. Lieblich, & D. McAdams (Eds.), *Up close and personal: The teaching and learning of narrative research* (pp. 259–274). Washington, DC: American Psychological Association.

Josselson, R., Lieblich, A., & McAdams, D. (2007). *The meaning of others: Narrative studies of relationships.* Washington, DC: American Psychological Association.

Kendall, G. & Wickham, G. (1999). *Using Foucault's methods.* London: Sage.

Kendall, G. & Wickham, G. (2007). The Foucaultian framework. In C. Seale, G. Gobo, J. Gubrium, & D. Silverman (Eds.), *Qualitative research practice* (pp. 129–138). London: Sage.

Krippendorff, K. (2004). *Content analysis: An introduction to its methodology* (2nd ed.). Thousand Oaks, CA: Sage.

Kristeva, J. (1980). *Desire in language: A semiotic approach to literature and art* (L. Roudiez, Ed.). (T. Gora, A. Jardine, & L. Roudiez, Trans.). New York: Columbia University Press.

Kristeva, J. (1982). *Powers of horror: An essay on abjection* (L. Roudiez, Trans.). New York: Columbia University Press. (Original work published 1980)

Kuno, S. & Kaburaki, E. (1977). Empathy and syntax. *Linguistic Inquiry, 8,* 627–672.

Kvale, S. (2007). *Doing interviews.* Los Angeles: Sage.

Labov, W. (1972). In Labov W. (Ed.), *Language in the inner city: Studies in the black English vernacular.* Philadelphia: University of Pennsylvania Press.

Labov, W. (1982). Speech actions and reactions in personal narratives. In D. Tannen (Ed.), *Analyzing discourse: Text and talk* (pp. 219–247). Washington, DC: Georgetown University Press.

Labov, W. (1997). Some further steps in narrative analysis. *Journal of Narrative and Life History, 7*, 397–415.

Labov, W. (2010). Where shall I begin? In D. Schiffrin, A. DeFina, & A. Nylund (Eds.), Telling stories: Language, narrative, and social life (pp. 7–22). Washington, DC: Georgetown University Press.

Labov, W. & Waletsky, J. (1967). Narrative analysis: Oral versions of personal experience. In J. Helm (Ed.), *Essays on the verbal and visual arts* (pp. 12–44). Seattle: American Ethnological Society/University of Washington Press.

Landman, J. (2001). The crime, punishment, and ethical transformation of two radicals: Or how Katherine Power improves on Dostoevsky. In D. McAdams, R. Josselson, & A. Lieblich (Eds.), *Turns in the road: Narrative studies of lives in transition* (pp. 35–66). Washington, DC: American Psychological Association.

Langellier, K. (1989). Personal narratives: Perspectives on theory and research. *Text and Performance Quarterly, 9*(4), 243–275.

Langellier, K. (2001). "You're marked": Breast cancer, tattoo and the narrative performance of identity. In J. Brockmeier & D. Carbaugh (Eds.), *Narrative identity: Studies in autobiography, self, and culture* (pp. 145–184). Amsterdam: John Benjamins.

Lather, P. & Smithies, C. (1997). *Troubling the angels: Women living with HIV/AIDS.* Boulder: Westview.

Lévi-Strauss, C. (1975). The raw and the cooked: An introduction to a science of mythology (J. & D. Weightman, Trans.). New York: Harper and Row.

Lieblich, A., McAdams, D., & Josselson, R. (2004). *Healing plots: The narrative basis of psychotherapy.* Washington, DC: American Psychological Association.

Lieblich, A., Tuval-Mashiach, R., & Zilber, T. (1998). *Narrative research: Reading, analysis, and interpretation.* London: Sage.

Lincoln, Y. & Guba, E. (1985). *Naturalistic inquiry.* Beverly Hills, CA: Sage.

Lofland, J. & Lofland, L. (1995). *Analyzing social settings: A guide to qualitative observation and analysis* (3rd ed.). Belmont, CA: Wadsworth.

Macbeth, D. (2001). On "reflexivity" in qualitative research: Two readings, and a third. *Qualitative Inquiry, 7*(1), 35–68.

MacIntyre, A. (2007). *After virtue* (3rd ed.). Notre Dame: University of Notre Dame.

Mandler, J. (1984). *Stories, scripts, and scenes: Aspects of schema theory.* Hillsdale, NJ: Lawrence Erlbaum.

Marshall, H., Woollett, A., & Dosanjh, N. (1998). Researching marginalized standpoints: Some tensions around plural standpoints and diverse "experiences". In K. Henwood, C. Griffin, & A. Phoenix (Eds.), *Standpoints and differences: Essays in the practice of psychology* (pp. 115–134). London: Sage.

Maruna, S. (1997). Going straight: Desistance from crime and life narratives of reform. In R. Josselson & A. Lieblich (Eds.), *The narrative study of lives* (pp. 59–93). Thousand Oaks, CA: Sage.

Mattingly, C. (1998). *Healing dramas and clinical plots: The narrative structure of experience.* Cambridge: Cambridge University Press.

Mattingly, C. (2005). Toward a vulnerable ethics of research practice. *Health: An Interdisciplinary Journal for the Social Study of Health, Illness, and Medicine, 9*(4), 453–471.

Mattingly, C. & Garro, L. (Eds.). (2000). *Narrative and the cultural construction of illness and healing.* Beverly Hills, CA: University of California Press.

McAdams, D. (1985). *Power, intimacy, and life story: Personological inquiries into identity.* New York: Guilford

McAdams, D. (2006). *The redemptive self: Stories Americans live by.* Oxford: Oxford University Press.

McAdams, D. (1993). *The stories we live by: Personal myths and the making of the self.* New York: William Morrow.

McAdams, D. (1999). Personal narratives and the life story. In L. Pervin & O. John (Eds.), Handbook of personality theory and research (2nd ed., pp. 478–500). New York: Guilford.

McAdams, D. (2003). Personological assessment: The life story of Madeline G. In J. Wiggins (Ed.), *Paradigms of personality assessment* (pp. 213–225). New York: Guilford Press.

McAdams, D. (2006). *The redemptive self: Stories Americans live by.* Washington, DC: American Psychological Association.

McAdams, D., Anyidoho, N., Brown, C., Huang, Y., Kaplan, B., & Machado, M. (2004). Traits and stories: Links between dispositional and narrative features of personality. *Journal of Personality, 72*(4), 761–784.

McAdams, D., Hoffman, B., Mansfield, E., & Day, R. (1996). Themes of agency and communion in significant autobiographical scenes. *Journal of Personality, 64*(2), 339–377.

McAdams, D. & Pals, J. (2006). A new big five: Fundamental principles for an integrative science of personality. *American Psychologist, 61*(3), 204–217.

McAdams, D. & West, S. (1997). Introduction: Personality psychology and the case study. *Journal of Personality, 65*(4), 757–783.

McLeod, J. (2001). *Qualitative research in counselling and psychology.* London: Sage.

McNamee, S. & Gergen, K. (Eds.). (1992). *Therapy as social construction.* London: Sage.

Merrill, B., & West, L. (2009). *Using biographical methods in social research.* Los Angeles: Sage.

Mills, C. W. (2000). *The sociological imagination: Fortieth anniversary edition.* New York: Oxford University Press.

Mishler, E. (1986a). *Research interviewing: Context and narrative.* Cambridge: Harvard University Press.

Mishler, E. (1986b). The analysis of interview-narratives. In T. Sarbin (Ed.), *Narrative psychology: The storied nature of human conduct* (pp. 233–255). New York: Praeger.

Mishler, E. (1995). Models of narrative analysis. *Journal of Narrative and Life History, 5*(2), 87–123.

Mishler, E. (1990). Validation in inquiry-guided research: The role of exemplars in narrative studies. *Harvard Educational Review, 60*(4), 415–442.

Mishler, E. (1991). Representing discourse: The rhetoric of transcription. *Journal of Narrative and Life History, 1*(6), 255–280.

Mishler, E. (1995). Models of narrative analysis. *Journal of Narrative and Life History, 5*(2), 87–123.

Mishler, E. (1997). The interactional construction of narratives in medical and life-history interviews. In B. Gunnarson, P. Linnell, & B. Nordberg (Eds.), *The construction of professional discourse* (pp. 223–244). London: Longman.

Mitchell, V. (2007). Earning a secure attachment style: A narrative of personality change. In R. Josselson, A. Lieblich, & D. McAdams (Eds.), *The meaning of others: Narrative studies of relationships* (pp. 93–116). Washington, DC: American Psychological Association.

Montgomery, K. (1991). *Doctors' stories: The narrative structure of medical knowledge.* Princeton: Princeton University Press.

Murray, M. (2003). Narrative psychology and narrative analysis. In P. Camic, J. E. Rhodes, & L. Yardley (Eds.), *Qualitative research in psychology* (pp. 95–112). Washington, DC: American Psychological Association.

Nicolopoulou, A. (1997). Labov's legacy for narrative research- and its ironies. *Journal of Narrative and Life History, 7*(1), 369–377.

Nussbaum, M. (1995). *Poetic justice: the literary imagination and public life.* Boston: Beacon Press.

Ochberg, R. (2003). Teaching interpretation. In R. Josselson, A. Lieblich, & D. McAdams (Eds.), *Up close and personal: The teaching and learning of narrative research* (pp. 113–134), Washington, DC: American Psychological Association.

Padgett, D. (2008). *Qualitative methods in social work research* (2nd ed.). Los Angeles: Sage.

Parker, J. (1992). *Discourse dynamics. Critical analysis for social and individual psychology.* London: Routledge.

Patterson, W. (2008). Narratives of events: Labovian narrative analysis and its limitations. In M. Andrews, C. Squire, & M. Tamboukou (Eds.), *Doing narrative research* (pp. 22–40). Sage: London.

Patton, M. (2002). *Qualitative research and evaluation methods* (3rd ed.). Thousand Oaks, CA: Sage.

Pels, D. (2000). Reflexivity: One step up. *Theory, Culture, and Society, 17*(3), 1–25.

Phoenix, A. (2008). Analysing narrative contexts. In M. Andrews, C. Squire, & M. Tamboukou (Eds.), *Doing narrative research* (pp. 64–77). Los Angeles: Sage.

Platt, J. (1992). "Case study" in American methodological thought. *Current Sociology, 40*(1), 17–48.

Plummer, K. (1995). *Telling sexual stories.* London: Routledge.

Poindexter, C. (2002). Meaning from methods. *Qualitative Social Work, 1*(1), 59–78.

Poindexter, C. (2003). Sex, drugs, and love among the middle aged: A case study of a serodiscordant heterosexual couple coping with HIV. *Journal of Social Work Practice in the Addictions, 3*(2), 57–83.

Poland, B. (2002). Transcription quality. In J. Gubrium & J. Holstein (Eds.), *Handbook of interview research: Context and method* (pp. 629–650). Thousand Oaks, CA: Sage.

Polanyi, L. (1985). Conversational storytelling. In T. van Dijk (Ed.), *Discourse and dialogue, vol. 3 of Handbook of discourse analysis 4* (pp. 183–201). London: Academic Press.

Polkinghorne, D. (1988). *Narrative knowing and the human sciences.* Albany: State University of New York.

Polkinghorne, D. (1995). Narrative configuration in qualitative studies. In J. Hatch & R. Wisniewski (Eds.), *Life history and narrative* (pp. 5–24). London: Falmer.

Polkinghorne, D. (2007). Validity issues in narrative research. *Qualitative Inquiry, 13*(4), 471–486.

Pomerantz, A. (1984). Agreeing and disagreeing with assessments: Some preferred/dispreferred turn shapes. In J. Atkinson & J. Heritage (Eds.), *Structures of social action: Studies in conversation analysis* (pp. 57–101). Cambridge: Cambridge University Press.

Potter, J. (2003). Discourse analysis and discursive psychology. In P. Camic, J. Rhodes, & L. Yardley (Eds.), *Qualitative research in psychology: Expanding perspectives in methodology and design* (pp. 73–94). Washington, DC: American Psychological Association.

Potter, J. (2004). Discourse analysis as a way of analysing naturally occurring talk. In D. Silverman (Ed.), *Qualitative research: Theory, method and practice* (2nd ed.) (pp. 200–221). London: Sage.

Potter, J. & Wetherell, M. (1987). *Discourse and social psychology.* London: Sage Publications.

Propp, V. (1968). *Morphology of the folktale* (L. Scott, Trans.). Austin: University of Texas. (Original work published 1928).

Ragin, C. (1992). Introduction: Cases of "What is a case?". In C. Ragin & H. Becker (Eds.), *What is a case? Exploring the foundations of social inquiry* (pp. 1–18). Cambridge: Cambridge University Press.

Ragin, C. & Becker, H. (Eds.). (1992). *What is a case? Exploring the foundations of social inquiry.* Cambridge: Cambridge University Press.

Ragin, C., Nagel, J., & White, P. (2004). *Report summary. Scientific foundations of qualitative research.* Arlington, VA: National Science Foundation.

Reason, P. & Bradbury, H. (Eds.). (2001). *Handbook of action research: Participative inquiry and practice.* Thousand Oaks, CA: Sage.

Ribeiro, B. T. (2006). Footing, positioning, voice. Are we talking about the same thing? In A. de Fina, D. Schiffrin, & M. Bamberg (Eds.), *Discourse and identity* (pp. 48–82). Cambridge: Cambridge University Press.

Ricoeur, P. (1991). Life in quest of narrative. In D. Wood (Ed.), *On Paul Ricoeur: Narrative and interpretation* (pp. 24–33). New York: Routledge.

Riessman, C. (1990). *Divorce talk: Women and men make sense of personal relationships.* New Brunswick, NJ: Rutgers University Press.

Riessman, C. (1993). *Narrative analysis.* London: Sage.

Riessman, C. (2008). *Narrative methods for the human sciences.* Thousand Oaks, CA: Sage.

Riessman, C. & Quinney, L. (2005). Narrative in social work: A critical review. *Qualitative Social Work, 4*(4), 391–412.

Riessman, C. & Speedy, J. (2007). Narrative inquiry in the psychotherapy professions: A critical review. In D. Clandinin (Ed.), *Handbook of narrative inquiry: Mapping a methodology* (pp. 426–456). Thousand Oaks, CA: Sage.

Roberts, B. (2002). *Biographical research.* Buckingham, UK: Open University Press.

Robinson, J. & Hawpe, L. (1986). Narrative thinking as a heuristic process. In T. Sarbin (Ed.), *Narrative psychology: The storied nature of human conduct* (pp. 111–125). New York: Praeager.

Robinson, W. (1951). The logical structure of analytic induction. *American Sociological Review, 16*, 812–818.

Rogers, A. (2007). The unsayable, Lacanian Psychoanalysis and the art of narrative. In D. Clandinin (Ed.), *Handbook of narrative inquiry: Mapping a methodology* (pp. 99–119). Thousand Oaks, CA: Sage.

Rogers, A., Casey, M., Ekert, J., Holland, J., Nakkula, V., & Sheinberg, N. (1999). An interpretive poetics of languages of the unsayable. *The Narrative Study of Lives, 6*, 77–106.

Rosenthal, G. (1993). Reconstruction of life stories: Principles of selection in generating stories for narrative biographical interviews. *The Narrative Study of Lives, 1*(1), 59–91.

Rosenthal, G. (Ed.). (1998). *The Holocaust in three generations.* London: Cassell.

Rosenwald, G. (2003). Task, process, and discomfort in the interpretation of life histories. In R. Josselson, A. Lieblich, & D. McAdams (Eds.), *Up close and personal: The teaching and learning of narrative research* (pp. 135–150). Washington, DC: American Psychological Association.

Roth, H. (1991). *Call it sleep.* New York: Farrar, Straus & Giroux. (Original work published 1934).

Runyan, W. (1980). Alternative accounts of lives: An argument for epistemological relativism. *Biography, 3*(3), 209–224.

Runyan, W. (1982). In defense of the case study method. *American Journal of Orthopsychiatry, 52(3),* 440–446.

Rustin, M., & Chamberlayne, P. (2002). Introduction: From biography to social policy. In P. Chamberlayne, M. Rustin, & T. Wengraf (Eds.), *Biography and social exclusion in Europe* (pp. 1–22). Bristol, UK: The Policy Press.

Sacks, H., Schegloff, E., & Jefferson, G. (1974). A simplest systematics for the organization of turn-taking for conversation. *Language, 50,* 696–735.

Said, E. (1990). American intellectuals and Middle East politics. In B. Robbins (Ed.), *Intellectuals: Aesthetics, politics, academics* (pp. 135–151). Minneapolis: University of Minnesota Press.

Sands, R. (2004). Narrative analysis: A feminist approach. In D. Padgett (Ed.), *The qualitative research experience* (pp. 48–75). Belmont, CA: Thomson Brooks/Cole.

Schiff, B. (2006). The promise (and challenge) of an innovative narrative psychology. *Narrative Inquiry, 16*(1), 19–27.

Schiff, B. & Noy, C. (2006). Making it personal: Shared meanings in the narratives of Holocaust survivors. In A. De Fina, D. Schiffrin, & M. Bamberg (Eds.), *Discourse and identity* (pp. 398–425). Cambridge: Cambridge University Press.

Schiffrin, D., Tannen, D., & Hamilton, H. (Eds.). (2001). *The handbook of discourse analysis.* Malden, MA.: Blackwell.

Schwandt, T. (2007). The pressing need for ethical education: A commentary on the growing IRB controversy. In N. Denzin & M. Giardina (Eds.), *Ethical futures in qualitative research: Decolonizing the politics of knowledge* (pp. 85–98). Walnut Creek, CA: Left Coast Press.

Sclater, S. (1998). Nina's story: An exploration into the construction and transformation of subjectivities in narrative accounting. *Auto/biography, 6,* 67–77.

Seale, C. (2002). Quality issues in qualitative inquiry. *Qualitative Social Work, 1*(1), 97–110.

Seale, C., Gobo, G., Gubrium, J., & Silverman, D. (2007). Part 2: Analytic frameworks. In C. Seale, G. Gobo, & D. Silverman (Eds.), *Qualitative research practice* (pp. 95–96). London: Sage.

Shaw, I. & Norton, M. (2008). Kinds and quality of social work research. *British Journal of Social Work, 38*(5), 953–970.

Shay, J. (1994). *Achilles in Viet Nam: Combat trauma and the undoing of character.* New York: Scribner.

Shuman, A. (2005). *Other people's stories: Entitlement claims and the critique of empathy.* Urbana: University of Illinois Press.

Silverman, D. (1993). *Interpreting qualitative data: Methods for analysing talk, text and interaction.* London: Sage.

Silverman, D. (1998a). *Harvey Sacks: Social science and conversation analysis.* New York: Oxford University Press.

Silverman, D. (1998b). Analyzing conversation. In C. Seale (Ed.), *Researching culture and society* (pp. 261–274). London: Sage.

Silverman, D. (2001). *Interpreting qualitative data: Methods for analyzing talk, text, and interaction.* London: Sage.

Silverman, D. (2004). Who cares about 'experience'? Missing issues in qualitative research. In D. Silverman (Ed.), *Qualitative research: Theory, method and practice* (second ed., pp. 342–367). London: Sage.

Singer, J. (2001). Living in an amber cloud: A life story analysis of a heroin addict. In D. McAdams, R. Josselson, & A. Lieblich (Eds.), *Turns in the road: Narrative studies of lives in transition* (pp. 253–278). Washington, DC: American Psychological Association.

Spence, D. (1986). Narrative smoothing and clinical wisdom. In T. Sarbin (Ed.), *Narrative psychology: The storied nature of human conduct* (pp. 211–232). New York: Praeger.

Spradley, J. (1979). *The ethnographic interview.* New York: Holt, Rinehart, & Winston.

Squire, C. (2005). Reading narratives. *Group Analysis, 38*(1), 91–107.

Squire, C. (2007a). *HIV in South Africa: Talking about the big thing.* London: Routledge.

Squire, C. (2007b). *Narrative research ISM301, Study Guide.* Unpublished manuscript.

Squire, C. (2008). Experience-centered and culturally-oriented approaches to narrative. In M. Andrews, C. Squire, & M. Tamboukou (Eds.), *Doing narrative research* (pp. 41–63). Los Angeles, CA: Sage.

Squire, C., Andrews, M., & Tamboukou, M. (2008). Introduction: What is narrative research? In M. Andrews, C. Squire, & M. Tamboukou (Eds.), *Doing narrative research* (pp. 1–21). Los Angeles: Sage.

Stake, R. (2000). Case studies. In N. Denzin & Y. Lincoln (Eds.), *Handbook of qualitative research* (2nd ed., pp. 435–454). Thousand Oaks, CA: Sage.

Stanford Encyclopedia of Philosophy Online. (2008). *Michel Foucault.* Retrieved May 1, 2009 from http://plato.stanford.edu/entries/foucault

Stoecker, R. (1991). Evaluating and rethinking the case study. *Sociological Review, 39*(1), 88–112.

Tamboukou, M. (2008). A Foucauldian approach to narratives. In M. Andrews, C. Squire, & M. Tamboukou (Eds.), *Doing narrative research* (pp. 102–120). London: Sage.

Todorov, R. (1990). *Genres in discourse.* Cambridge: Cambridge University Press.

van der Merwe, C. & Gobodo-Madikizela, P. (2008). *Narrating our healing.* Newcastle, UK: Cambridge Scholars Publishing.

van Dijk, T. (Ed.). (1985). *The handbook of discourse analysis.* London: Academic Press.

Van Manen, M. (1990). *Researching lived experience: Human sciences for an action-sensitive pedagogy.* New York: State University of New York Press.

Wells, K. (December, 2007). The experience of custody loss: Preliminary narrative analysis of one mother's report. Invited presentation at the Chapin Hall Center for Children, University of Chicago, Chicago IL.

Wells, K. (2010). A narrative analysis of one mother's story of child custody loss and regain. *Children and Youth Services Review,* doi: 10.1016/j.childyouth.2010.06.019

Wengraf, T. (2001). *Qualitative research interviewing: Biographic narrative and semi-structured methods.* London: Sage.

West, C. (1989). *The American evasion of philosophy.* Madison: University of Wisconsin.

White, M. (2007). *Maps of narrative practice.* New York: W. W. Norton.

White, M. & Epston, D. (1990). *Narrative means to therapeutic ends.* New York: W. W. Norton.

White, S. (2001). Auto-ethnography as reflexive inquiry: The research act as self-surveillance. In N. Gould & I. Shaw (Eds.), *Qualitative research in social work* (pp. 100–115). London: Sage.

Wiggins, S. & Potter, J. (2008). Discursive psychology. In C. Willig & W. Stainton-Rogers (Eds.), *The Sage handbook of qualitative research in psychology* (pp. 73–90). London: Sage.

Wiggins, S., Potter, J., & Wildsmith, A. (2001). Eating your words: Discursive psychology and the reconstruction of eating practices. *Journal of Health Psychology, 6*(1), 5–15.

Wiley, N. *Bakhtin's voices and Cooley's looking glass self.* Retrieved April 21, 2009, from http://www.unlv.edu/centers/cdclv/pragmatism/wiley_bakhtin.html

Willig, C. (2001). *Introducing qualitative research in psychology: Adventures in theory and method.* Buckingham, UK: Open University Press.

Willig, C. (2003). Discourse analysis. In J. Smith (Ed.), *Qualitative psychology: A practical guide to research methods* (pp. 159–183). London: Sage.

Willig, C. (2008a). *Introducing qualitative research in psychology: Adventures in theory and method* (2nd ed.). Berkshire, England: Open University Press.

Willig, C. (2008b). Discourse analysis. In J. Smith (Ed.), *Qualitative psychology* (2nd ed.) (pp. 160–184). Los Angeles: Sage.

Wodak, R. (2001). The discourse-historical approach. In R. Wodak & M. Meyer (Eds.), *Methods of critical discourse analysis* (pp. 63–94). London: Sage.

Wodak, R. (2007). Critical discourse analysis. In C. Seale, G. Gobo, J. Gubrium, & D. Silverman (Eds.), *Qualitative research practice* (pp. 185–201). London: Sage.

Wolf, M. (1992). *A thrice told tale: Feminism, postmodernism and ethnographic responsibility.* Stanford: Stanford University Press.

Woodside-Jiron, H. (2004). Language, power, and participation: Using critical discourse analysis to make sense of public policy. In R. Rogers (Ed.), *An introduction to critical discourse analysis in education* (pp. 173–205). Mahwah, New Jersey: Lawrence Erlbaum Associates.

Wortham, S. (2000). Interactional positioning and narrative self-construction. *Narrative Inquiry, 10,* 157–184.

Wortham, S. (2001). *Narratives in action: A strategy for research and analysis.* New York: Teachers College Press.

Yin, R. (2003). *Case study research: Design and methods* (3rd ed.). Thousand Oaks, CA: Sage.

Index

CPSIA information can be obtained
at www.ICGtesting.com
Printed in the USA
BVOW10s0843130417

481142BV00006B/45/P